Creating Restorative Justice

Creating Restorative Justice

A Communication Perspective of Justice, Restoration, and Community

Gregory D. Paul and Ian M. Borton

LEXINGTON BOOKS
Lanham • Boulder • New York • London

Published by Lexington Books
An imprint of The Rowman & Littlefield Publishing Group, Inc.
4501 Forbes Boulevard, Suite 200, Lanham, Maryland 20706
www.rowman.com

6 Tinworth Street, London SE11 5AL, United Kingdom

British Library Cataloguing in Publication Information Available

Library of Congress Cataloging-in-Publication Data

Names: Paul, Gregory D., 1981- author. | Borton, Ian M., 1979- author.
Title: Creating restorative justice : a communication perspective of justice, restoration,
    and community / Gregory D. Paul and Ian M. Borton.
Description: Lanham : Lexington Books, 2021. | Includes bibliographical references and
    index. | Summary: "The authors argue that communication plays a central role in the
    evolution of different frameworks of restorative justice. Not just about sending and
    receiving messages, communication gives meaning to restorative justice and helps
    to structure thought and behavior when individuals engage in restorative practices in
    various contexts"—Provided by publisher.
Identifiers: LCCN 2021004069 (print) | LCCN 2021004070 (ebook) |
    ISBN 9781498576451 (cloth) | ISBN 9781498576475 (paperback) |
    ISBN 9781498576468 (epub)
Subjects: LCSH: Restorative justice. | Communities—Social aspects.
    Classification: LCC HV8688 .P378 2021 (print) | LCC HV8688 (ebook) |
    DDC 364.6/8—dc23
LC record available at https://lccn.loc.gov/2021004069
LC ebook record available at https://lccn.loc.gov/2021004070

Contents

Preface

As we write this text, protests have exploded around the United States as police officers in Minnesota have been charged with a number of crimes related to the death of George Floyd. A wide array of protesters, with slogans such as "no justice, no peace," are speaking out and acting to counter systemic racism against African Americans by police and also against racism in other systems, including healthcare, the economy, and the legal system more broadly. Meanwhile, COVID-19, which emerged only months before, has had a disproportionately negative impact on minority communities both in terms of health and economic impacts in the form of job losses and unemployment (Centers for Disease Control and Prevention, 2020). Anger has spilled over into violence, as some look to quite literally tear down systems seen as oppressive, racist, and unfair. Injustice is at the heart of the experiences and stories of George Floyd, Ahmaud Arbery, Breonna Taylor, Philando Castille, and many others in our recent and distant pasts. As we write about justice, injustice, and restorative justice, it is impossible to separate our discussion from what we hope will be the seeds of meaningful systemic change going forward.

Acknowledgments

This book has been the fruition of a journey we began together over a decade ago at a National Communication Association conference. Over that time, we've shared that journey with a good many others who have contributed to our learning and practice of restorative justice.

We would like to express our deep thanks and acknowledge the support of departmental colleagues, with whom we have shared ideas and questions over the years; colleagues in the National Communication Association, including Amanda Feller, Eddah Mutua, Jessica Jameson, and Bill Donohue; and the people within the community organizations we have been fortunate to work with over the years. We are grateful for the guidance and support in ways large and small over the years of this book's writing, editing, and production. You all have helped to shape our thinking, spark our curiosity, and deepen our practice of restorative justice and communication over the years.

Introduction

From a young age, we are socialized into a network of beliefs, values, and norms pertaining to ourselves, one another, our relationships, our communities, and the world at large. We're told what's good and bad, right and wrong, appropriate and inappropriate, true and false. These lessons, taught at home, in schools, and in communities, are reinforced as we see and experience consequences for abiding by or violating those rules and expectations. We learn not only what we are supposed and not supposed to do but also what happens as a consequence of those behaviors. We also become sensitized to situations when we believe someone is doing something to us that they shouldn't. Moreover, these justice-related beliefs, values, and norms become connected to questions about identity, relationships, and belonging. These beliefs, values, and norms evolve as we experience the world around us and make sense of those experiences. Our journey through the world is a function of intertwined worldviews, relationships, sense-making, contexts, and experiences.

But what happens when we encounter something on our journey that we believe to be unfair or harmful? How do we come to believe that something is unfair? How do we try to address those situations? What are the individual, relational, and communal consequences of our attempts to address them? How do we evaluate the effectiveness, appropriateness, and fairness of those attempts to address? In many ways, these questions are at the heart of a moral concept that underlies and shapes much of our journey: the concept of justice.

Just as our journeys through the world are complex and evolving, so too are our understandings of what justice means and looks like. Although we often use words like "fairness" and "equality" as synonyms for justice, justice is a multi-faceted concept with definitions that vary by person, by context, and over time. Kelley (2016), for example, describes four principles of outcome-related justice in relationships: equity, or distribution of goods based on effort; equality, or distribution of goods evenly across partners; needs-based, or distribution of goods based on need; and processual, or fair treatment. In organizational contexts, justice is conceptualized as having at least four dimensions: distributive, which is concerned with how outcomes are allocated; procedural, which is concerned with the fairness of the procedures used to determine outcomes; interactional, which is concerned with the fairness of interpersonal treatment; and informational, which is concerned with the appropriateness of information used.

Justice not only has multiple dimensions, but also has wide-ranging influence on our lives, shaping how we make sense of ourselves, our relationships, and our communities. For example, the group value model of justice (Konovsky, 2000; Lind & Tyler, 1988; Tyler & Lind, 1992) theorizes that the way people are treated clues them into their status within a group. This is especially important in light of the problems of racism, sexism, and other forms of discrimination that essentially communicate to groups of people that they are "less than" others. Further, people's beliefs about how others should be treated are shaped by their conceptualizations of justice. This is evident when we see calls for wrongdoers to be punished to the full extent of the law based on the just-world hypothesis (Lerner, 1980) that negative behavior should receive negative consequences. We have likely learned such responses from a young age, when we experienced punishment as a consequence for doing something we should not have done. This, then, is the vicious cycle of punitive justice—we learn at a young age that wrongdoing is met with punishment, which we carry into adulthood and apply in other areas of our lives, including our families, schools, workplaces, and communities. Yet, the flip side, captured by actor-observer bias, is that when we engage in wrongdoing, we attribute it to external causes while asking for mercy for ourselves. In other words, justice is a relational and symbolic concept that is fraught with complications, tensions, and contingencies. That is, it is a very human concept.

Perhaps it is no surprise, then, that the related concept of restorative justice is just as fraught (Paul & Borton, 2017). Considerable energy has been devoted to defining what restorative justice means in terms of its principles (e.g., peace, participation, healing, and accountability), processes (e.g., dialogue, circles, victim-offender mediation), and outcomes (e.g., multidimensional restoration as determined by the victim). Yet, while we value that work and find important meaning in it, we are less interested in refereeing or judging than in taking a descriptive posture that recognizes and investigates different approaches to and contexts of restorative justice. This posture is shaped not only by our experiences as facilitators and mediators but also by our academic backgrounds. As communication scholars, we are particularly sensitive to the roles that communication plays in making restorative justice what it is. We argue that restorative justice is a social construct and that a communication perspective—one that focuses on the relational and symbolic nature of human communication—can both inform and enhance the ways in which we practice, research, and evaluate restorative justice.

It is this communication perspective that structures our approach to restorative justice throughout this book. Drawing on conventional and constitutive perspectives of communication (Craig, 1999), we highlight the communicative foundations of restorative justice approaches that emphasize processes and programs (i.e., the proceduralist approach) and those that emphasize systems and structure change (i.e., the structuralist approach). Understanding communication as constituting our social realities through discourse and interaction (Fairhurst & Putnam, 2004), we approach the diverse definitions, processes, and practices of restorative justice not as problems but rather as outgrowths of our situated communication, our socialization, and the very nature of social construction.

This constitutive perspective of communication guides our approach to constructing this text of restorative justice. Chapters 1 and 2 focus on the communicative foundation of justice, focusing on evolving stories of justice and tracing those to contemporary justice practices and definitions. Chapters 3–6 drill down into contexts in which restorative justice is being practiced— in families, schools, communities, and the digital world. Chapter 7 examines evaluations of restorative justice and the stories we tell ourselves about what's "working" and how we tell whether or not it's "working." Threaded throughout are stories and experiences from practitioners whom we interviewed as part of this project. Together, we hope that these reported experiences give evidence of a practices and conceptualizations that are continuously evolving and transforming as conditions and contexts change.

REFERENCES

Fairhurst, G. T., & Putnam, L. (2004). Organizations as discursive constructions. *Communication Theory, 14*(1), 5–26. https://doi.org/10.1111/j.1468-2885.2004. tb00301.x.

Kelley, D. L. (2016). *Just relationships: Living out social justice as mentor, family, friend, and lover*. Routledge.

Konovsky, M. A. (2000). Understanding procedural justice and its impact on business organizations. *Journal of Management, 26*(3), 489–511. https://doi.org/10.1016/S 0149-2063(00)00042-8.

Lerner, M. (1980). *The belief in a just world: A fundamental delusion*. New York: Plenum.

Lind, E. A., & Tyler, T. R. (1988). *The social psychology of procedural justice*. Plenum.

Paul, G. D., & Borton, I. M. (2017). Toward a communication perspective of restorative justice: Implications for research, facilitation, and assessment. *Negotiation and Conflict Management Research, 10*(3), 199–219. https://doi.org/10.1111/ncmr.12097.

Tyler, T. R., & Lind, E. A. (1992). A relational model of authority in groups. In M. P. Zanna (Ed.), *Advances in experimental social psychology* (Vol. 25, pp. 115–191). Academic Press.

Chapter 1

A Communication Perspective of Restorative Justice*

I think of the obvious things like fairness and determining things for the overall good, having goodness as your goal, and doing it in a fair way that treats people equally. But one aspect of justice, I think, is people seeing things through their own eyes and not through the eyes of others; hearing with their own ears, and not the ears of others. So getting away from the whole, people trying to manipulate and influence other people, whether it's how to decide something, how to vote, how to spend their money, whatever. But getting people to think for themselves, but not with their own interest in mind, thinking for themselves, but for the good of everyone as a whole. And everyone meaning, what's the situation? Are you dealing with a family situation? Are you dealing with a situation in your village? Is it a national situation or a world situation like global warming or something of that nature?—Restorative Justice Practitioner

It's more of an overarching feeling that things are balanced, that what I have to say matters as well as what you have to say. And what happens to me, you recognize that that's a harm and so you're gonna work with me to figure out how to make that right. It's not about punishing. It's not about pointing fingers and making sure one person is the only one being held responsible for things. . . . I see justice if you look at it as a bigger overarching theme. That's what justice is: looking at making sure that it's all addressed and there's a balance in when something happens.—Restorative Justice Practitioner

It just depends. I hate that, but it just depends on the person, on the situation. I think often, justice is personally, for me, it's viewed as a good outcome based on what I think is a good outcome. And do I feel

---

* Interviews at the beginning: The identities of the interviewees from the author's interviews have been anonymized.

5

like I've been given justice? I don't know, I just don't have a good definition. I'm so sorry.—Restorative Justice Practitioner

A MEANINGFUL JOURNEY

As we start this journey, let's take a moment to think about the people in your life with whom you are particularly close. What is it that you value about your relationships with them? How do they make you feel? How do you talk with them, and what do you talk about? How does this compare with your relationships and interaction with people to whom you're not particularly close? What about with people you don't know in society at large? How do you work through those challenging times in which you feel hurt by something someone else has done or that you've done to them? How were you socialized to respond, act, and interact in such situations? What were your goals in working through those situations? In all likelihood, threaded throughout your answers to these questions are beliefs about right and wrong, identity, relationships, and ways of being in and moving through the world. These beliefs aren't simply contained within these discrete relationships—they are connected to your many daily experiences and interactions, from the mundane to the extraordinary.

Such stories are part of the human experience, the personal journey that shapes how we make sense of ourselves, our relationships, and our world. They set the stage for our expectations for how we should be treated, how we should (and should not) respond to hurtful situations, and how we want to engage with others around us. Our stories and the stories we hear of others come together to create a network of beliefs, values, and norms pertaining to ourselves, one another, our relationships, our communities, and the world at large. Through stories, we learn about good and bad, right and wrong, appropriate and inappropriate, true and false. These lessons are reinforced as we observe and experience consequences for abiding by or violating those rules and expectations. In many ways, our daily experiences shape and are shaped by our values, beliefs, attitudes, and norms about the interconnected concepts of justice (what is fair?), morality (what is right?), identity (who am I?), characterization (who are you?), relationships (who are we?), and belonging (should I be here?) (Clayton & Opotow, 2003; Okimoto, Wenzel, & Feather, 2009; Zehr, 2002). They evolve as we experience the world around us, adapt to changing situations, and make sense of our surroundings and selves—all necessary components of our journey. This journey is constituted by intertwined, socially constructed worldviews, relationships, sense-making, contexts, experiences, and stories, all of which have something in common: they are imbued with meaning.

This emphasis on meaning-making is intentional. It focuses our attention not just on people but also on people's interpretations, interaction, and engagement and the larger social consequences of those symbols and interpretations (Giles, 2019; Schiff & Hooker, 2019). It asks us to explore not only what people say to one another and how they say it but also what people *make* through that communication, viewing our world as co-constructed through conversation (Pearce & Pearce, 2000). This includes moral systems, of which justice is a part, that emerge through dialogue and relationships (Waldron & Kelley, 2008). It asks us to pay attention not only to the intrapersonal/cognitive but also to the interpersonal/social and the systemic/structural. It asks us to consider developing a new language or grammar of justice and restorative justice that will facilitate growth (Schiff & Hooker, 2019). In short, it asks us to take seriously that which gives meaning to our journey—communication (Kellett & Dalton, 2001).

Highlighting communication brings to the fore several questions about justice and restorative justice. For example, how do we come to interpret something as being unfair? How are these interpretations shaped by our contexts and experiences? What happens if our interpretations differ from the interpretations of others? How do our interpretations influence how we try to address those situations? How do we negotiate the meanings not only of the behavior but also of ourselves, our relationships, and our communities? What are the individual, relational, and communal consequences of our attempts to address them? How do we evaluate the effectiveness, appropriateness, and fairness of those attempts? How do those attempts at justice create larger systems that shape our action and interactions? In many ways, these questions of meaning, shaped through communication, are at the heart of the concept of justice.

CONSTRUCTIONS OF JUSTICE

Just as our journeys through the world are complex and evolving, so too are our interpretations of justice. Although we often use words like "fairness" and "equality" as synonyms for justice, justice is a multi-faceted concept with definitions that vary by person, by context, and over time (Kelley, 2016; Paul, 2015a, 2015b; Vaandering, 2011; Warnke, 1992). For example, Kelley (2016) argues that social justice plays a key role in shaping our interpretation of our relationships, asserting that people evaluate the fairness of relationships using four criteria: (a) equity, or distribution of goods based on effort; (b) equality, or distribution of goods evenly across partners; (c) needs-based, or distribution of goods based on need; and (d) processual, or fair treatment. In organizational contexts, justice has been conceptualized as having at least four dimensions: distributive, which is concerned with the fairness of outcomes; procedural, which is concerned with the fairness of the procedures used to determine outcomes; interactional, which is concerned with the fairness of interpersonal treatment; and informational, which is concerned with the appropriateness of information used (Colquitt, 2001). In legal contexts, at least in the West, justice is connected largely with fairness of process and fairness of outcomes. In terms of process, the concept of procedural justice refers to the importance and implications of following fair processes. Procedural justice theories assert that people will view authoritative systems, such as the police and the court system, as being legitimate if they follow appropriate procedures (Rossner, 2013; Tyler, Sherman, Strang, Barnes, & Woods, 2007). Procedural justice in legal settings involves treating all parties in accordance with rules and procedures that have been laid out ahead of time. In terms of outcomes, consequences are typically seen as fair if they match the severity of the offending behavior that gave rise to them. Such outcomes are largely punitive (e.g., "justice is served") (McCold & Wachtel, 2002; Okimoto, Wenzel, & Feather, 2009; Paul & Dunlop, 2014; Wenzel & Okimoto, 2009; Zehr, 2002), leading conventional justice to be framed by many restorative justice scholars as "retributive justice" (Allena, 2004; Armour & Umbreit, 2007; Wachtel & McCold, 2002; Wenzel, Okimoto, & Cameron, 2012; Wenzel, Okimoto, Feather, & Platow, 2010; Zehr, 2002).

Interpretations of justice have wide-ranging influence on our lives, shaping how we make sense of ourselves, our relationships, and our communities. For example, the group value model of justice (Konovsky, 2000; Lind & Tyler, 1988; Tyler & Lind, 1992) theorizes that people make sense of their status and belonging within groups based on the ways they are treated. Poor treatment by others may be interpreted as signaling that one has low status within the larger social group or that others do not value the individual or their relationship. From this perspective, harmful treatment is not only a violation of norms but also is a violation of one's *identity* or self-concept (Wenzel & Okimoto, 2010; Zehr, 2002b). As Zehr (2002b) writes, "When we become victims, the experience calls into question our most fundamental assumptions about who we are, who we can trust, and what kind of world we live in. These include our assumptions about the orderliness of the world, our sense of autonomy or personal control, and our sense of relatedness—where we fit in a web of social relationships" (p. 23). Likewise, social identity shapes perceptions of justice (Sargeant, Antrobus, Murphy, Bennett, & Mazerolle, 2016). In short, injustice is inherently about *meaning*—our meaning inherently and relative to others. If we believe that we have been marginalized, it is all too natural to want to reciprocate and demand negative consequences for the wrongdoer (Okimoto et al., 2009). This motivation increases as severity and perceived intentionality increase. Thus, whether the wrongdoing is episodic or structural, it is normative (at least in the West) to seek justice in the form of punishing or bringing suffering to the perceived perpetrators in order to "rebalance" the scales, reaffirm community norms for appropriate behavior, and reassert our identities and ideologies that have emerged and taken shape through our interactions and experiences.

It is with this attention to communication and meaning that we approach *restorative justice*. For years, scholars and practitioners have debated, deliberated, and dialogued about restorative justice through research articles, treatises, monographs, interviews, websites, and more trying to define what restorative justice means. One commonly cited definition of restorative justice comes from Marshall (1999), who defines restorative justice as "a process whereby parties with a stake in a specific offense collectively resolve how to deal with the aftermath of the offense and its implications for the future" (p. 5). Bazemore and Walgrave (1999), in turn, define restorative justice as "every action that is primarily oriented toward doing justice by repairing the harm that has been caused by a crime" (p. 48). Paul (2015a) defines it as "a theory of justice that emphasizes the restoration of individuals, relationships, and communities following behavior perceived as harmful, offensive, or problematic" (p. 100). At its base, restorative justice is concerned with accomplishing restoration (or the rectifying of wrongs) along multiple dimensions (relational, material, financial, and moral), typically through direct, facilitated dialogue between affected stakeholders (typically victims, wrongdoers, and their supporters).

Definitions of restorative justice wrestle with a number of questions: Is it individual or relational? Is it limited to legal systems or does it apply to larger social systems? Is it oppositional to (or complementary to) conventional justice? What or who gets "restored"? What is "justice" in the first place? Is it concerned primarily with the harmed person, the harm-doer, or both? What is the role of the larger community in which injustice occurs? These questions are connected to one another and to various contexts—social, political, legal, economic, cultural, ideological, and more—comprising an entire system of justice beliefs.

We do not claim to have the *right* answer to any of these questions. Instead, we approach restorative justice from more of a descriptive, deliberative posture that foregrounds the role of communication (Ryfe, 2011). We argue that communication, meaning, and discourse are fundamental to the conceptualization, practice, exploration, and evaluation of restorative justice and that taking communication perspectives can inform, enhance, and enrich the theoretical, research, and practical dimensions of restorative justice. In short, the questions that continue to emerge about restorative justice are functions of ways we interpret symbols like "justice" and "restoration," of contexts in which we study and practice restorative justice, of related concepts such as identity, and of intersecting dynamics such as power, race, and conflict.

WHAT DO WE MEAN BY
COMMUNICATION PERSPECTIVES?

There are multiple communication perspectives that can shape interpretations and practices of restorative justice (Craig, 1999). Perhaps the most common perspective taken in the restorative justice literature is also the most conventional: the cybernetic or transmission perspective (e.g., Borton & Paul, 2015; Riley & Hayes, 2018; Willis & Hoyle, 2019). This perspective, exemplified by the sender message channel receiver (SMCR) model of communication, focuses on the flow and effect of verbal and nonverbal messages between senders and receivers. (For example, when people use the word "communications" [with an "s"], they likely are working from this transmission model of communication.) The SMCR model is useful for a range of questions pertaining to processes, outcomes, and advocacy. For example, what types of apologies are provided in victim-offender mediations, and to what extent are they effective? What effect does talk time shared by the parties have on outcome and process perceptions of restorative justice processes? How do facilitators communicate during restorative processes, and what effects do those communication practices have on outcome and process perceptions? What types of messages are most effective at developing positive attitudes toward restorative justice? Such questions are both interesting and informative in terms of improving training, practice, and advocacy.

Another perspective—the constitutive perspective—draws attention to other communicative layers and dynamics related to meaning, interpretations, and structures. This constitutive perspective, exemplified by coordinated constitution of meaning (CCM) (Pearce, 1995), underlies the framing of restorative justice as a social construct constituted by stories, symbols, and language systems (Kellett & Dalton, 2001). From this perspective, people, relationships, and the world are always in a state of becoming, shaped through our interactions and interpretations, which are both products and producers of the systems of which we are a part (Pearce & Pearce, 2000). It is through communication that people socially construct their realities as they implicitly and explicitly negotiate what things mean through their everyday discourses and interaction (Fairhurst & Grant, 2010). Such negotiation and strategic framing is connected with underlying power bases and ideologies and can have a variety of outcomes. For example, reframing "crime" as "harm" highlights the personal consequences of wrongdoing and the inadequacy of impersonal mechanisms that constitute the Western conventional legal system for addressing those consequences. Language is not neutral.

This means that the diverse definitions, processes, and practices of restorative justice are not problems but rather are simply functions of situated, strategic communication, and socialization: the very nature of social construction. It also surfaces both different questions and different methods to answer those questions. For example, as we've noted elsewhere (Paul & Borton, 2017), it asks us to examine "microelements of negotiation, dynamic ebbs and flows of conflict, and meaning systems apparent in language" (p. 215). This more descriptive posture helps us to explore *how* and *why* people communicate, emote, and interact when they meet; deploy language strategically to accomplish goals; and use communication to (re-)negotiate power. This constitutive perspective also asks us to see researchers and practitioners (ourselves included) as rhetoricians making arguments about the merits and nature of restorative justice, meaning that we can deconstruct texts, analyze them through critical lenses, and draw interpretations about the evolution of restorative justice's meaning(s). Moreover, we can situate restorative justice as a part of larger social systems, meaning that we can position restorative justice as making communities, relationships, and people what they are.

A CONSTITUTIVE PERSPECTIVE
OF RESTORATIVE JUSTICE

This constitutive perspective of communication is at the heart of our exploration of the framing of restorative justice. Given the complex histories of justice within various social groups, it is no wonder that modern scholars and practitioners have spent considerable effort defining restorative justice, delineating its contexts, and debating its boundaries (e.g., Braithwaite & Strang, 2001; Daly, 2016; Gavrielides, 2006; Johnstone, 2002; Johnstone & Van Ness, 2013; McCold, 2000, 2004; McCold & Wachtel, 2002; Roberts, 2010). These efforts center on understandings and assumptions about what constitutes "justice," what is being "restored," and in what contexts restorative justice is being practiced (Paul & Borton, 2017).

While these discussions may seem removed from the day-to-day practice of restorative justice, we argue here and elsewhere (Paul & Borton, 2017) that they are consequential to the growth, evolution, practice, evaluation, and advocacy for restorative justice. Paul and Dunlop (2014), for example, identify outcomes ranging from material restitution to human and relational growth that are associated with restorative justice, while Paul and Borton (2013) explore the different ways facilitators make sense of restorative justice and facilitation. This diversity is interesting both observationally and practically. From a constitutive perspective, the discursive diversity of restorative justice shapes such growth, evolution, practice, evaluation, and advocacy. In other words, the way people frame restorative justice makes restorative justice what it is. Thus, far from being inconsequential, definitions of restorative justice are central to and inseparable from the practice of restorative justice.

This conceptual variation suggests that restorative justice is a fluid, adaptive, and contested idea (Gavrielides, 2008). While some exploration of those contestations is helpful, we focus more on the implications of the divergent ways in which academics and practitioners frame, or give meaning to, restorative justice. We approach this meaning-making activity as an ongoing conversation about what restorative justice *should* be—a combination of the aspirational and the actual (Kurki, 2003). These aspirational and actual conversations not only constitute restorative justice but also shape how we practice it, how we evaluate it, and with whom we partner to carry it out.

THE EMERGENCE OF PROCEDURALIST
AND STRUCTURALIST FRAMEWORKS

Paying attention to specific language choices reveals an interesting evolution in the work of restorative justice. For example, Green, Johnstone, and Lambert (2013) write:

> As knowledge and awareness of restorative justice has grown, so too has its application. Alongside restorative "justice," there is increasingly restorative "practice" or restorative "approaches." This change in language signifies a new stage in the evolution of restorative justice as it moves beyond the repair of harm caused by criminal conduct to addressing problems in schools, social services, workplaces, and neighborhoods. (p. 445)

The evolution in language suggests the emergence of at least two frameworks for restorative justice. One framework, what we call the *proceduralist framework*, aligns with "purist" conceptualizations of restorative justice in that it focuses rather narrowly on restorative justice as a criminal justice concept focused on healing victims' harms wrought by offenders' illegal behavior. The other framework, the *structuralist framework*, aligns more with "maximalist" conceptualizations of restorative justice in that it focuses more broadly on using restorative practices to achieve social justice and restoration in light of historical harm wrought by society at large.

These are not necessarily mutually exclusive approaches, even though they are sometimes treated as such as people strategically look to direct the work of restorative justice in ways that align with their set of interests and ideologies. Rather, they represent themes or vocabularies—framing work— in how people talk about and practice restorative justice. Particularly within structuralist discourses, there tends to be a clear articulation of the benefits and consequences of structuralist and proceduralist approaches. For example, Wachtel and McCold (2001) argue:

> If systems are not inherently restorative, they cannot hope to effect change through an occasional restorative intervention. Restorative practices must be systemic, not situational. You can't just have a few people running conferences

and everybody else doing business as usual. You can't be restorative with students but retributive with staff. You can't have restorative policy and punitive courts. To reduce the growing negative subcultures inside and outside corporate life, to successfully prevent crime and to accomplish meaningful and lasting change, restorative justice must be perceived as a social movement dedicated to making restorative practices integral to everyday life. (p. 129)

This interest in the development of a social movement of restorative justice is at the heart of the proceduralist / structuralist distinction. In the following sections, we explore this distinction and its implications for practice (table 1.1).

FRAMING RESTORATIVE JUSTICE

At its core, restorative justice is concerned with making right something that has been put wrong. This is embedded in the root terms of "restorative" and "justice." To restore implies the occurrence of some wrong, typically called "harms," "wrongs," "offenses," and "injustices." "Justice," in turn, implies a sense of fairness, or things/people being in the state they should be relative to themselves, others, and their communities. Together, the concepts imply an emphasis on that which was harmed—whether they be people, relationships, or larger systems—being returned to (and existing in) an appropriate, fair, and just state, and that which did the harming—again, whether they be people, relationships, or larger systems—being accountable and responsible for making right that which was harmed. What becomes tricky, though, is that the ways in which these concepts are framed suggests different ways of restoring justice.

Table 1.1.   Comparison of Proceduralist and Structuralist Approaches to Restorative Justice

	Proceduralist	*Structuralist*
Type of harm	Criminal	Historical, social
Justice emphasis	Procedural justice	Social justice
Conceptual scope	Purist, narrow	Maximalist, broad
Practices	VOM/VOC	Circles, practices
Level of focus	Individual	Macro
Historical roots	Kitchener	Indigenous
Practical orientation	Programs	Movement
Outcomes sought	Individual Reparation	Individual and social change

Source: Author created.

Exigency for Restorative Justice

In conflict research, "sparking events" (Bies, Tripp, & Kramer, 1997; Paul, 2015) are those events that initiate or set off perceptions of conflict due to their violation of some expectation, value, or belief. In the case of restorative justice, sparking events are those events, actions, or practices that are interpreted as being offensive, harmful, and unjust. Such interpretations are rooted in diverse individual, relational, and cultural histories (Paul, 2016), meaning that what one person interprets as being unjust may be interpreted by another person as simply "different" or "the way things are." From social inequality and violations of social norms, interpretations of something as being "harmful" are functions of interrelated frameworks of language, power, position, and more. These types of harm—from the individual to the system—provide the first point of divergence between proceduralist and structuralist frameworks of restorative justice.

Proceduralists and structuralists tend to focus on two different types of injustice, even if they are not mutually exclusive. (In fact, a strong argument can be made that individual and systemic injustice are products and producers of one another.) On the one hand, proceduralists tend to focus on discrete, personal offenses that have happened in the relative short-term. Such offenses typically include crimes, inappropriate treatment (e.g., bullying), or a similar negative event that has happened in the relatively recent past. In these situations, the harm done (e.g., the sustaining of a material, physical, or emotional injury) can typically be at least somewhat readily identified, even if not necessarily easily addressed. For example, behavior such as vandalism, theft, and simple assault are typically identified by an authority figure who defines the nature of the offense, such as when prosecutors press particular charges, managers accuse someone of a particular offense, or teachers suspend a student for a particular reason. These definitions serve to frame behavior such that there is a single way to interpret the nature of the wrongdoing (i.e., naming) and a clear distinction between offender and victim (i.e., blaming). Such naming and blaming, which are functions of what we might call "bracketing" of the situation, have implications for what should be done to rectify the situation. Such bracketing entails putting clear boundaries or edges around the behavior, such that everything not within the brackets is typically considered irrelevant or not as relevant as what is within the brackets. In conventional justice settings, for example, jurors are instructed to examine and weigh only that information that exists within the brackets, regardless of what may have led to it. In this way, restorative justice advocates argue that processes such as victim-offender conferencing, victim-offender mediation, family group conferencing, and circles are superior to conventional practices in that they give participants control over where to place the brackets and how to interpret what is in bounds and what is out of bounds.

Structuralists, on the other hand, tend to expand the types of harms addressed through restorative practices. Often referred to as "historical harms" or "social harms" (Karp & Frank, 2016), these wrongs include systemic harms such as racism, sexism, gender discrimination, and economic suppression. While such discrimination can be operationalized or exemplified by pointing to particular events, the focus more so tends to be on the systemic nature of harms and the impact of that discriminatory and harmful system on a group of people. This does not mean that this framing ignores specific, recent harms; rather, it is that it tends to situate such harms historically and socially. This has a number of implications. For one, all individuals within the system are positioned as having a stake in the restorative process. For another, this broader understanding of harm and the experience of it tends to invite a wide range of actions to be considered as possible responses and encourages attention be paid not only on the recent past but also on the more distant pasts of individuals, relationships, and communities.

In some ways, this focus on recent versus historical harms aligns with espoused histories of restorative justice. The Kitchener experiment in 1974, in which police in Ontario took two teenagers who had vandalized property door to door to apologize for their behavior, tends to be identified as the springboard for more modern restorative justice programs (Bonta, Wallace-Capretta, Rooney, & Mcanoy, 2002; Peachey, 1989). The experiment, as well as the work of Mennonite and other groups, led to the creation of a number of programs throughout North America that used similar (but more formalized) processes, such as victim-offender mediation and victim-offender conferencing, as people looked for better ways to address juvenile offending (Zehr, 2002). Yet, structuralists trace the roots of restorative justice back much farther (see chapter 2), highlighting ancient, indigenous roots of restorative justice (Lewis & Umbreit, 2015) and pointing to evidence of restorative justice values and practices in social systems of people groups stretching back centuries or more (e.g., the Maori people group (Moyle & Tauri, 2016). As Zehr (2002) notes, modern restorative justice efforts "[owe] a special debt to the Native people of North America and New Zealand. The precedents and roots of restorative justice are much wider and deeper than the Mennonite-led initiatives of the 1970s. Indeed, they are as old as human history" (pp. 11–12). Highlighting its evidence in social systems also enhances the argument for expanding the use of restorative principles and practices beyond just the criminal justice system and into all facets of life. We suggest in the next chapter that these two historical starting points may be more entwined. A story of restorative justice may begin with indigenous practices, enter into broader public discourse through Kitchener, before being "returned" to the very same communities from whence it came.

In short, the divergence in proceduralist and structuralist framing shapes and is shaped by their claimed histories. These histories, in turn, help to focus practitioners' and researchers' attention on types of harms to be addressed by restorative justice efforts. One consequence of these differing histories and sensitivities is that there may be a mismatch in terms of who "counts" as victims and offenders. For example, someone working from a structuralist framework and focusing on systemic harms related to sexism may argue that a certain demographic or social group may be complicit in creating systems of sex-based discrimination. However, someone operating from a proceduralist perspective may not see themselves as being complicit in that they have not actively or intentionally engaged in sex-based discrimination. These two frameworks may create conflict and an inability to collaborate in restorative advocacy. Moreover, the two frameworks tend to include different types of activities and approaches as being a part of restorative justice, only some of which may align across frameworks.

Restoring Justice

McCold (2000) explores and distinguishes a number of processes identified as falling under the umbrella of restorative justice. These processes occur in multiple contexts, including the criminal justice system, schools, families, and nation-states (Borton, 2016; Green, Johnstone, & Lambert, 2013; Johnson & Johnson, 2012; Karp, 2004; Kidder, 2007; Morrison, 2006; Paul & Riforgiate, 2015; Roche, 2003; Shaw, 2007; Wunsttin, 2001). One of the points of contention (or "fault lines" as termed by Gavrielides, 2008) addressed by McCold is whether all of these processes should be counted as restorative justice. Both McCold and Zehr (2002) argue that processes can be placed along a continuum from "fully restorative" to "partly" or "pseudo" restorative, based on the extent to which they hold to restorative principles. For McCold, those principles are victim reparation, offender responsibility, and communities of care reconciliation. For Zehr (2002), those principles are the focus on harms and needs, obligation through accountability and responsibility, and engagement through participation in restorative processes. Based on the Venn diagram created, McCold argues that the only processes that are "fully restorative" are peace circles, family group conferencing, and community conferencing. Similarly, Zehr (2002) identifies victim offender conferences, circles, and family group conferences as reflecting restorative principles. These delineations are reflective of a "purist" approach to restorative justice that draws a narrower boundary around what counts as restorative justice, although Zehr's focus on principles tends to blur or loosen those boundaries. In contrast, "maximalist" approaches are more inclusive in terms of what counts as restorative justice. The variance in inclusiveness is evident in both the language used and outcomes emphasized.

One shift in the ways in which practitioners talk about what they do is the use of the term "restorative practices." This term typically refers to a wide range of support practices aimed toward helping youth and adults experience healing following trauma. These practices are especially prevalent in schools, where counselors, teachers, administrators and outside groups aim to help and train youth and school officials on how to do restorative justice. This "whole school restorative justice" approach (e.g., Davis, 2018; González, Sattler, & Buth, 2019) is emblematic of structuralist framings of restorative justice that focus on change at the collective level that transcends organizational systems and then influences individuals. This may be contrasted to a focus on change at the individual level that may or may not result in larger societal change. On a larger scale, this structuralist approach to restorative justice is akin to a social movement that aims to accomplish social, economic, political, and cultural restoration (Johnstone & Van Ness, 2013; Wachtel & McCold, 2001).

The proceduralist approach to restorative justice, however, tends to be more limited in that it focuses on the implementation of specific programs to accomplish individual change. Such approaches are especially prevalent in the context of the criminal justice system, in which units are established within the court system to encourage (typically youth) offenders take responsibility for their behavior and provide reparation to their victims through victim-offender mediation or conferencing. These programs tend to offer a rather narrow set of processes designed to accomplish a narrowly defined set of outcomes.

The implication of these differences in processes is that the approaches tend to pursue and foreground different outcomes. Commonly assessed outcomes in restorative justice include individual-level outcomes such as victim satisfaction and offender recidivism. The prevalence of these outcomes, assessed by organizations through post-program surveys to demonstrate effectiveness, reflects a proceduralist approach to restorative justice that primarily emphasizes individualized conceptualizations of justice and restoration.

Yet, there is some dissatisfaction with the emphasis on these "objective" outcomes. Emerging from this dissatisfaction is an increasing push to consider the more intangible individual outcomes as well as larger, societal-level outcomes. Individual outcomes included empowerment, learning how to resolve conflict, getting questions answered, and transforming offenders' lives. Societal/relational outcomes included blending control with social support, creating "a restorative city where restorative justice is predominant," "shifting societal views of justice," and greater empathetic understanding. If there is a common theme among these outcomes, it is the sense that even these intangible individual outcomes will eventually lead to a more equal, understanding social network in which people are able to come together, work through conflict, and maintain community.

IMPLICATIONS

Scholars and practitioners continue to negotiate the meanings of restorative justice across multiple contexts. We do not argue that this negotiation is negative or problematic, although some undoubtedly want to settle the matter once and for all. Instead, from our communication perspective, we argue that conceptual differences in the frameworks of restorative justice are products of deeply rooted, socially constructed differences in what *justice* means, what *restoration* means, and what exactly is being restored. Whereas the proceduralist framework is quite conventional (at least from a Western perspective) in terms of its focus on quantifiable, individual outcomes achieved through programs implemented as part of the current justice system, the structuralist framework conceives of restorative justice as underlying a social justice movement in which restorative practices are used to accomplish broader systemic change in response to current and historical harms.

We contend that these differences have several implications for perceived legitimacy, practice, and assessment of restorative justice. In terms of legitimacy, one of the first hurdles restorative justice practitioners must overcome is raising awareness of what restorative justice is. It is in this description of restorative justice where they must work to align their conceptualization of restorative justice with their audience's values, beliefs, and norms regarding people, relationships, and society as a whole. Individuals with an aversion to social justice language or ideologies may be turned off by more structuralist descriptions but may be more receptive to programs that frame their work as supporting victims, reducing recidivism, and improving the criminal justice system. However, audiences who are more supportive of social justice goals and who are more critical of conventional criminal justice system inequities may resist conventional proceduralist descriptions and instead gravitate toward those restorative justice programs they see as addressing the roots of fundamental, societal problems. Thus, organizational representatives aiming to build symbolic and financial support for their work would do well to be sensitive to frame alignment through their language.

These differences also have implications for what practices are considered to fall under the umbrella of restorative justice. Are conflict resolution training programs that work with youth considered restorative? Are community dialogue programs that address discrimination restorative? Are victim-offender mediation programs restorative *enough*? Moreover, approaches also have implications for where practitioners aim to house their programs. Do they house them within the criminal justice system, which will likely reduce programmatic offerings and limit program aims? What kind of relationship (antagonistic? collaborative? partnered?) do practitioners build with the conventional system? Who else do organizations work with as partners? How practitioners make sense of what restorative justice means will shape their answers to all of these questions.

Framing will also impact how practitioners evaluate the effectiveness of their work. Proceduralist organizations likely turn to more conventional outcomes that are more traditionally measured (e.g., satisfaction and recidivism). These limited, short-range assessments resonate with the individual-level goals of these programs that exist within conventional systems and serve to maintain their legitimacy (and funding) from those systems. Structuralist approaches, though, have a bit of a harder time establishing their effectiveness, in part because they are trying to accomplish larger-scale social change. Because cultural change is a years-long effort, such organizations tend to point to the ongoing work they are doing—number of workshops, types of populations engaged in the work, stories of participants—to demonstrate that they are continuing the ongoing work of social change.

In all, examining the framing of restorative justice highlights the different ways people define and practice restorative justice. This divergence between the more narrowly defined proceduralist approach and the more broadly defined structuralist approach is evident in how practitioners talk about justice, restoration, and the work of restoring justice. It also has implications for how organizations function as they carry out, evaluate, and build support for their work among external stakeholders. As research in this area continues, it would be beneficial for scholars and practitioners to acknowledge and discuss the assumptions they are making about their work, about one another, and their ideal outcomes. Doing so can help to grow the work of restorative justice by helping all parties understand, make room for, and support the diverse practices of restorative justice in all its incarnations.

REFERENCES

Bazemore, G., & Walgrave, L. (1999). Restorative justice: In search of fundamentals. In G. Bazemore & L. Walgrave (Eds.), *Restorative juvenile justice: Repairing the harm of youth crime* (pp. 45–74). Criminal Justice Press.

Borton, I. M., & Paul, G. D. (2015). Problematizing the healing metaphor of restorative justice. *Contemporary Justice Review, 18*(3), 257–273. https://doi.org/10.1080/10282580.2015.1057704.

Centers for Disease Control and Prevention. (2020). *COVID-19 in Racial and Ethnic Minority Groups*. U.S. Dept. of Health and Human Services.

Clayton, S., & Opotow, S. (2003). Justice and identity: Changing perspectives on what is fair. *Personality and Social Psychology Review, 7*(4), 298–310. https://doi .org/10.1207/S15327957PSPR0704_03.

Colquitt, J. A. (2001). On the dimensionality of organizational justice: A construct validation of a measure. *Journal of Applied Psychology, 86*(3), 386–400. https://do i.org/10.1037/0021-9010.86.3.386.

Craig, R. T. (1999). Communication theory as a field. *Communication Theory, 9*(2), 119–160. https://doi.org/10.1111/j.1468-2885.1999.tb00355.x.

Fairhurst, G. T., & Grant, D. (2010). The social construction of leadership: A sailing guide. *Management Communication Quarterly, 24*(2), 171–210. https://doi.org/10 .1177/0893318909359697.

Kelley, D. L. (2016). *Just relationships: Living out social justice as mentor, family, friend, and lover*. Routledge.

Konovsky, M. A. (2000). Understanding procedural justice and its impact on business organizations. *Journal of Management, 26*(3), 489–511. https://doi.org/10.1016/S 0149-2063(00)00042-8.

Lerner, M. (1980). *The belief in a just world: A fundamental delusion*. New York: Plenum.

Lind, E. A., & Tyler, T. R. (1988). *The social psychology of procedural justice*. Plenum.

Marshall, T. F. (1999). *Restorative justice: An overview*. Home Office, Research Development and Statistics Directorate.

Okimoto, T. G., Wenzel, M., & Feather, N. T. (2009). Beyond retribution: Conceptualizing restorative justice and exploring its determinants. *Social Justice Research, 22*, 156–180. https://doi.org/10.1007/s11211-009-0092-5.

Paul, G. D. (2015a). Predicting participation in victim offender conferences. *Negotiation and Conflict Management Research, 8*(2), 100–118. https://doi.org/10 .1111/ncmr.12049.

Paul, G. D. (2015b). Justice perceptions and practices of restorative justice facilitators and the public. *Contemporary Justice Review, 18*(3), 274–295. https://doi.org/10.1 080/10282580.2015.1057678.

Paul, G. D. (2016). A bona fide group perspective of restorative justice: Implications for researchers and practitioners. In P. M. Kellett & T. G. Matyok (Eds.), *Transforming conflict through communication in personal, family, and workplace relationships* (pp. 125–130). Lexington Books.

Paul, G. D., & Borton, I. M. (2017). Toward a communication perspective of restorative justice: Implications for research, facilitation, and assessment. *Negotiation and Conflict Management Research, 10*(3), 199–219. https://doi.org/10.1111/ncmr .12097.

Pearce, W. B. (1995). A sailing guide for social constructionists. In W. Leeds-Hurwitz (Ed.), *Social approaches to communication* (pp. 88–113). Guilford.

Pearce, W. B., & Pearce, K. A. (2000). Extending the theory of the coordinated management of meaning (CMM) through a community dialogue process.

Communication Theory, 10(4), 405–423. https://doi.org/10.1111/j.468-2885.2000.
tb00200.x.
Tyler, T. R., & Lind, E. A. (1992). A relational model of authority in groups. In M. P.
Zanna (Ed.), *Advances in experimental social psychology* (Vol. 25, pp. 115–191).
Academic Press.
Vaandering, D. (2011). A faithful compass: Rethinking the term restorative justice to
find clarity. *Contemporary Justice Review, 14*(3), 307–328. https://doi.org/10.1080
/10282580.2011.589668.
Waldron, V., & Kelley, D. (2008). *Communicating forgiveness.* Sage.
Warnke, G. (1992). *Justice and interpretation.* The MIT Press.
Zehr, H. (2002). Journey to belonging. In E. G. M. Weitekamp & H-J Kerner (Eds.),
Restorative justice: Theoretical foundations (pp. 21–31). Willan.

Chapter 2

The Return of Restorative Justice

The story of Western justice practices finds its roots deep in Neolithic tribes, Egyptian gods, and the Aristotelian ship of state. Accompanying it is the theory and practice of restorative justice. Several researchers claim contemporary restorative justice practices stem from indigenous practices in cultures from Africa to Canada to New Zealand (Skelton, 2007; Willemsens & Walgrave, 2007; Wright, 1991). Claims made to restorative justice's traditional, indigenous roots are well documented. Braithwaite (1999), for instance, asserts that "restorative justice has been the dominant model of criminal justice throughout most of human history for all the world's peoples" (p. 1). The work goes on to cite traditions from all over the globe in support of the thesis. However, far from the idealized version sometimes put forward as evidence of restorative justice's enlightened pre-state past, actual tribal practices frequently addressed only relationships within members of the tribe. Strangers or members of neighboring tribes could expect to be robbed or even killed without pretext; they had no rights (Pratt, 2006).

In this chapter, we examine some of the claims presented by a variety of reviews/summaries of restorative justice programs around the world. In particular, we consider traditional systems' claims to *restorativeness* in terms of (a) process, (b) stakeholder involvement, and (c) program operations. These claims will then be examined in light of several theories, which may explain why traditional systems of indigenous justice repeatedly claim restorative justice paradigms as their own. Second, recent literature in criminology, sociology, communication, and penology have all commented (with differing amounts of praise or condemnation) on the globalization of crime control policy (Tauri, 2014; 2017). Through the historical processes of western colonialism and subsequent cultural globalization, the western model of jurisprudence has found purchase in communities and cultures far from its European

origin. Finally, we conclude by claiming that the same globalization processes, which took western justice across the world, have been operating in
recent decades to bring restorative practices back to the very communities in
which they are said to have begun. Linguistic barriers sometimes make comparing and contrasting claims to *restorativeness* difficult. What seems clear
at this point is that a wide (both in terms of geography and culture) variety
of claimants find the origins of restorative practices in their own respective
backyards (Johnstone & Van Ness, 2007).

Africa. The Tanzanian model of "conflicts as property" was first articulated
academically by Christie (1977, p. 1). According to this assessment, conflicts
belonged to the people in conflict, not to the systems of judicial, legal, or
police administration. The Tanzanian model has been further described as
"victim-oriented, with appropriate reparation by the offender" (Skelton, 2007,
p. 468). This model of justice communicates the willingness of participants
to share forgiveness with human sympathy (*ubuntu* or *utu*) (Skelton, 2007).

Asia. Across Asia, a number of non-state justice systems operate to address
tribal and ethnic group disputes (Gao, 2003; Golub, 2003; Ota, 2003). Jiang
and Yang (1990) also claim restorative justice's roots lie in Confucianism.
Parties are encouraged to settle disputes, to assist others in their conflicts and
to work toward settlement. Wang, Di, and Wan (2007) concede that while
the term "restorative justice" is new to Asia, they claim it is nevertheless
intimately woven into Asian culture (p. 477). Historically, courts were the
option of last resort in traditional Asian villages, whose citizens preferred to
employ an informal system dispute resolution. The challenge of translation
is apparent here as well, as Clarke (1991) notes that the term "mediation" in
China represents a process in which the goals underpinning laws, policies,
and governmental actions are articulated to participants in an effort to con-
vince them to comply. This is a more persuasive form of mediation than we
might be accustomed to in the west. It might include education or even overt
criticism while remaining a malleable process of compromise and allowance.
In Indonesia, customary law (*hokum adat*) helps maintain peace and "facilitates the informal dispute settlement process between offenders, victims, and
community" (Wang, Di, & Wan, 2007, p. 480). Finally, the Japanese cultural
emphasis on confession, repentance, and remorse has focused their restorative practices toward victim impact classes and victim awareness programs
(Haley, 1994).

The Americas. The earliest academic considerations of restorative justice in the Americas led researchers to explore victim-offender reconciliation, mediation, and sentencing circles. In particular, the circles model was
informed by first-nations justice (Van Ness, 2007). For these nations, circles
were a method of maintaining or restoring harmonious community connection. Circles could be used for solving the problems associated with

misbehavior while reaffirming traditional tribal norms. Restorative circle practices, learnt from First Nations peoples, also appealed to a number of American Christian denominations. Nowhere was this truer than with communities of Mennonites. Under the direction of Howard Zehr, a modified circle method would become the first Victim Offender Reconciliation Program.

Oceania. Half a world away, cultures of the Pacific islands also claim restorative justice as theirs (Maxwell & Hayes, 2007). In Polynesia and Melanesia, there is a well-documented history of extended family and village-level dispute resolution meetings. The process involves the community in a role of negotiation, collaboration, and compromise (Dinnen, 2003). Compensation, in the symbolic form of *ifoga*, also includes apology and attempts at reconciliation (Maxwell & Hayes, 2007). For the Maori of New Zealand, family and community meetings also reflect restorative justice practices and values. Eventually, Maori need for a justice model, which aligned more closely with their cultural traditions, was honored and legislated as the Children, Young Persons and Family Act of 1989. This act decentralized the justice process, "making some sort of reconciliation between offender and victim (usually with the payment of goods or services from the former to the latter with an apology) as the main focus of the justice 'event' " (Pratt, 2006, p. 58).

From Africa, to Asia, to the Americas and the islands in between, a host of cultures claim restorativeness in their roots. There are several theories that help to explain why so many indigenous practices incorporate the central tenets of restorative justice as their own. Morrison (2005) states, "There is not a single theoretical model that specifies the mechanism through which restorative justice is meant to work" (p. 29). Regardless, we believe there should be a more substantial consideration of how theories of communication help explain the seeming global ubiquity of restorative themes and practices.

In almost all cultures, one key use of interpersonal communication is to fill the foundational need of conforming to social expectations (Giffin & Patton, 1971). This might be as simple as social recognition (i.e., acknowledging a person's humanity and existence). However, because restorativejustice often operates in the wake of a social transgression (e.g., crime, wrongdoing), interpersonal communication likely reflects a more constitutive communicative process. In the aftermath of socially inappropriate behavior, the communication inherent to a restorative process has the ability to serve a vital function. Giffin and Patton (1971) assert "changes in a relationship need to be identified and affirmed" (p. 46). If an event (e.g., bullying, cheating, theft) causes the nature of the relationship to change or to be called into question, any subsequent communication needs to address those changes. Restorative processes enable participants to address those questions through dialogue to redefine their relationship.

Examined through a more rationalistic (and specifically economic) lens, the theory of social exchange posits that in relationships, humans act to maximize rewards and minimize costs (Littlejohn & Foss, 2008). According to this theory, a relationship is a series of interdependent and self-interested exchanges (Galvin, 2011). Interpersonal decisions are presented as a balance of rewards and costs. For example, crime and other misbehavior can be thought of as a societal and relational cost. The relational damage that occurs as a result of offending behavior is another cost of being in a relationship. Responding to the inevitable transgressions of interpersonal interactions is another cost. According to social exchange theory, rational actors will seek to minimize the costs of redressing offenses (Thibaut & Kelley, 1959) and will calculate whether relationships are still "worth it" based on whether the benefits exceed the costs. Social exchange theory can help explain cultures whose traditional justice practices mirror those of restorative justice. Such systems' rewards include member inclusion, reintegration, and relational repair. For these traditional justice practices, these rewards seem less costly than a system of justice prioritizing policing, incarceration, or exclusion.

However, the rationality of this theory cannot overlook the importance of the capacity for sanction and punishment in any system of justice. While descriptively restorative, ancient justice practices often do maintain social exclusion, punishment beatings, and other corporal sanctions frowned upon by most postmodern practitioners. Perhaps this is why apology remains such a frequently noted feature of restorative practices. As Axelrod (1984) comments, a particularly effective apology is more than a functional attempt to prevent retribution. Instead, apology communicates an individual's recognition of ethical regret for having damaged trust. It then goes further in attending to the possibility that someone's identity or their relationship with another might have been damaged (Axelrod, 1984).

The final theory we wish to consider is also probably the most widely cited in connection to restorative practices: *reintegrative shaming*. Posited in a seminal book, Braithwaite (1989) used observations drawn from New Zealand and Australia to connect restorative justice with community functioning. According to this theory, when family and community members direct shame at an offender, that shame could have powerful effects, so long as "it [is] done with a context of respect for the offender and [is] followed by efforts to reintegrate them" (Johnstone, 2002, p. 4). According to Braithwaite (1989), most Western communities had lost this potentially transformative method of social control. However, theorists also caution that shaming practices can easily backfire if the target judges the shaming to be an unjust humiliation (Pruitt & Kim, 2004). Thus, for reintegrative shaming to have the desired effect, it must avoid what Braithwaite (1989) terms "stigmatization." Such stigmatization results in offenders' (self)-exclusion and their desire to commune with similarly excluded individuals, making deplorable actions into badges of pride and honor.

Effective restorative practices are theorized to communicate to offenders condemnation of particular behaviors, rather than castigation of the individual. Respected others in the community separate the behavior from the offender. (In Christian parlance, hate the sin; love the sinner.) It is possible for shame to be both communicated and subsequently discharged. In this way, restorative practitioners hope to avoid the potential of offender emotional or physical self-harm, retaliatory attacks on others, avoidance, or withdrawal (Morrison, 2005). For Braithwaite and other proponents, reintegrative shaming holds the key to explaining not only the ubiquity of restorative practices in indigenous cultures but also the fundamental mechanisms by which modern restorative practices organize, operate, and generate their outcomes.

We believe in the insights gleaned from examining interpersonal communication, social exchange theory, and reintegrative shaming. They each provide a valuable framework for exploring restorative dynamics of justice processes. There seems to be a human need for the recognition and acknowledgment of significant others, rationality in our relationships, and reintegration into our valued communities.

THE GLOBALIZATION OF JUSTICE

Globalization has led to a greater sharing of trade, culture, and technology. Along with these, some Western justice practices have also been spread globally. International cooperation and coordination are nothing new for justice systems and can trace their origins to the West's history of colonialism. "Piracy and slavery, for example, have always been considered crimes against the international society" allowing states to prosecute offenders regardless of where their acts were committed (Udombana, 2003, p. 56). From then until now, the necessity for and convenience of sharing of standards of justice have grown more complex.

The globalization of justice's modern history can be traced to the 1948 adoption of the UN Universal Declaration of Human Rights (UDHR). Forty-eight nations agreed to its adoption; none voted against. Among its articles are the rights of the accused to an impartial and public tribunal to determine both the accused's rights and obligations (Article 10) and the presumption of innocence (Article 11). Article 1 of the document, however, lays out perhaps the most restorative of aspirations, imploring that all human beings "should act towards one another in a spirit of brotherhood" (Assembly, 1948). Meanwhile, the majority of the academic criminological literature "focused on macro-level theorizing about whether such globalization exists, and if so, its extent, scale, and impact" (Tauri, 2017, p. 46).

Scholarly critiques of the globalization of justice practices seem concerned with their connection with neoliberal economic policies (Chazal, 2013; Moghadam, 2009; Urbina & Álvarez, 2016; Wenzelburger, 2016; Wonders, 2016). Ideologically, neoliberalism links consumerism with the promotion of free-market economic policies where rational processes drive the social life (Urbina & Álvarez, 2016). Beginning in the 1970s and 1980s, the World Bank and International Monetary Fund set policy conditions for countries receiving new loans ostensibly aimed at confronting government corruption and liberalizing trade policy (Moghadam, 2009). By this, larger and more powerful economies extort favorable economic policies which benefit themselves, at the cost of smaller, economically dependent nations (Chazal, 2013; Wonders, 2016). The reforms required in order to receive loans via these organizations often entails moving to a more Western-style justice system.

Powerful international entities (e.g., the World Bank and International Monetary Fund [IMF]) counter that their policies have led to the expansion of human rights considerations, increased interdependence, contractual certainty, and a more stable rule of law (Udombana, 2003). In their eyes, the reforms required for further IMF loans are necessary to ensure the just and proper allocation of the funds, rather than enriching the lives of corrupt politicians and bureaucrats. Globalized justice reforms, the proponents assert, have helped to usher in an age of civilized cosmopolitan democracy (Udombana, 2003). When it comes to justice practices, the globalization of the Western model gravitates toward stricter, more centralized systems focused on law-and-order responses to offending behavior, while moving farther away from smaller, local community policing (LaChappelle, 2014; Wenzelburger, 2016).

As states adopt more Western practices of justice, there are notable shifts in both their societies and economies resulting in increased inequality, higher crime rates, and a cultural shift toward risk-taking (Wenzelburger, 2016). Punishments in such societies can become harsher and more punitive (Downes & Nelkin, 2011; Garland, 2001; Muncie, 2011). Urbina and Álvarez (2016), for example, criticize American penalization practices as "a mechanism of power and control through criminalization and penal expansion" (p. 45).

Critiques of globalization have rightly focused on the inequitable economic policies undergirding its operation. However, caught up in globalization's ethos are the promises, dreams, and expectations for the fair practice of justice. These aspirations are captured in optimistic declarations, which evoke our shared human experiences. The founding document of the International Criminal Court describes the bonds of our common humanity as a "delicate mosaic," which "may be shattered at any time" (United Nations, 1999).

Knowing that the bonds of our common humanity will be perpetually challenged, bent, broken, and ignored, what promises do more restorative practices offer? Can restorative justice help in creating systems and experiences more akin to the "connected, open, and accessible world" globalization promises (Chazal, 2013, p. 711)? To look at how systematized, governmentally (and institutionally) supported restorative justice looks like, we need look no further to Canada's Youth Criminal Justice Act (YCJA) of 2012.

The goal of Canada's YCJA was to minimize the juvenile court system while providing a broad spectrum of "community-based non-custodial interventions for midrange offenders" (Mann, 2014, p. 59). Incarceration was for violent or repeat juvenile offenders only. Originally, the YCJA did not mitigate charges for those aged fourteen or older who committed serious crimes, although this was later amended in 2008. The explicit purpose of the program was to provide juveniles with a consequential, rehabilitative, and reintegrative experience for the benefit and protection of their communities (Bala, Carrington, & Robert, 2009).

However, a conservative backlash a mere five years after its passage amended the program to place community protection and offender accountability ahead of rehabilitative or preventative services (Mann, 2014). The YCJA's initial focus was transmuted to a focus on deterrence through punishment, denunciation, and pre-trial detention. This process seems to capture what Garland (2000) first identified as a global turn toward more punitive measures (Mann, 2014; Meyer & O'Malley, 2005; Wenzelburger, 2016).

Thus, in the pendulum swing of culture, progressive efforts to shift juvenile justice toward a more restorative paradigm were fairly quickly responded to with a punitive turn, reflecting an increased focus on sentence length and punishment. Conservative critiques on the power of the apologetic, therapeutic attitude toward criminal behavior resulted in a "What Works" approach, highlighting retribution and incapacitation (Garland, 2001).

The cultural tug-of-war between retribution and restoration continued, with offenders, victims, and communities left in the middle. According to Wenzelburger (2016), socioeconomic variables tended to encourage politicians to "implement harsher policies" (p. 592). While, at the same time, research efforts (see Bottrell, 2007; Bracken Deane, & Morrisette, 2009; Bryne & Trew, 2008; Haigh, 2009; Hasley, 2009) seem to support a more restorative approach. They indicate "that transitions from persisting in crime to desisting are contingent on the coming together of meaningful attachments with prosocial others that foster changes in identity" (Mann, 2014, p. 61). While restorative justice seems to be supported by many such research results, without consideration of a number of additional, extra-programmatic factors, even restorative justice's legislative victories (like YCJA) may falter and ultimately prove unsustainable. Even when policies are enacted to foster the institutionalization of more restorative programs, they remain subject to the winds of political will, which highlights the important connection between proceduralist/programmatic and structuralist/systemic approaches to restorative justice and the importance of the framing of wrongdoing and justice.

Canada's YCJA is just one example of an attempt to institutionalize restorative justice onto a primarily punitive framework. Its example provides a number of lessons for those interested in the wider-scale adoption of restorative justice into existing justice programs/systems. First, contexts have different potentials (or ripeness) for restorative practice adoption depending on social, political, economic, legal, and cultural systems. Second, implementing restorative justice may be perceived as a threat to the currently entrenched systems, programs, organizations, and ideologies. Thus, trade-offs and tension are likely to occur and must be negotiated on an ongoing basis when restorative justice programs are developed, proposed, implemented, and evaluated. While some stakeholders may be pleased with the development of restorative programs, the give-and-take may leave other stakeholders experiencing loss, frustration, jealousy, resentment, or vindictiveness toward restorative justice programs. Third, there are a host of normative, analytical, and evaluative issues, which should be considered whenever a restorative program is under consideration for adoption. Failing to consider and then to address these issues can have dire ramifications for program sustainability. Programs lacking in stability or longevity ultimately fail to achieve the primary restorative justice goals of relational repair, community participation, multidimensional restoration, and offender accountability. When working to develop restorative justice initiatives, there are a number of contextual conditions which make program persistence more feasible.

First, restorative justice initiatives flourish better in contexts where consensual dispute resolution practices are normative. Thus, initiatives begun among the Maori, First Nations peoples of North America, Africa, and Australia likely will have an easier time than those begun in Europe, for example. Second, Tonry (2006) sees such initiatives having an easier time succeeding in "relatively non-politicized criminal justice policy-making processes" (p. 2). Third, restorative justice programs tend to flourish in contexts with a relatively strong separation of political powers, particularly in constitutionally based political systems. Finally, and perhaps most distressingly for individuals hoping to develop and sustain restorative justice programs in the United States, Tonry (2006) claims that such programs are more likely to take root in countries and contexts with a relatively sparing use of incarceration.

If that assessment is true, then we can reasonably expect restorative justice programs in states with higher incarceration rates (e.g., Louisiana, Oklahoma, and Mississippi, with rates of incarceration per 100,000 citizens at 1,082,

983, and 962, respectively) to face greater challenges than states with the lowest incarceration rates (e.g., Maine, Minnesota, and Massachusetts, with rates of incarceration per 100,000 citizens at 285, 289, and 318 respectively) (Glaze & Kaeble, 2013). Moreover, in addition to the constraints placed on restorative programs coming from the political and judicial contexts, jurisdictions with "highly moralistic attitudes toward crime or with traditions of imposing very harsh punishments" will also find the adoption of restorative justice initiatives comparatively difficult (Tonry, 2006, p. 22).

CONCLUSION

Together, these features suggest the need for symbolic convergence or overlap between restorative justice programs and the wider systems in which they operate. Notwithstanding these potential frustrations, we find ourselves in a complex society full of moral imagination. With restorative justice, more can be done to "address the needs of injured parties for attention, protection, compensation and so forth than in classical criminal proceedings" (Boutellier, 2006, p. 41). A civil society requires the norms of a rules-governed system of justice, crime response, and a focused ethic of communication, which serves to legitimize and reinforce the validity of punitive actions (Mannozzi, 2002). The limited, instrumental value of a normatively punitive system can be enhanced with restorative elements, which treat offenders as co-equal moral subjects (Boutellier, 2006).

We have shown how, to varying degrees, many indigenous practices of justice claim restorativeness in their roots. However, most of these practices have been circumvented, lost, or quashed by globalization and the reach of Western justice practices. It is only in the past few decades have those same Western practices have begun to incorporate restorative justice into their responses to crime and offending behavior.

REFERENCES

Assembly, U. G. (1948). Universal declaration of human rights. *UN General Assembly*.

Axelrod, R. (1984). *The evolution of cooperation*. New York: Basic Books.

Bala, N., Carrington, P. J., & Roberts, J. V. (2009). Evaluating the Youth Criminal Justice Act after five years: A qualified success. *Canadian Journal of Criminology and Criminal Justice*, *51*(2), 131–167.

Bottrell, D. (2007). Resistance, resilience and social identities: Reframing "Problem Youth" and the problem of schooling. *Journal of Youth Studies*, *10*(5), 597–616.

Boutellier, H. (2006). Vital context of restorative justice. In Ivo Aertsen, Tom Daems, & Luc Robert (Eds.), *From Institutionalizing Restorative Justice* (pp. 25–43). Willan: Portland.

Bracken, D. C., Deane, L., & Morrissette, L. (2009). Desistance and social marginalization: The case of Canadian Aboriginal offenders. *Theoretical Criminology, 13*(1), 61–78.

Braithwaite, J. (1989). *Crime, shame and reintegration.* Cambridge University Press.

Braithwaite, J. (1999). Restorative justice: Assessing optimistic and pessimistic accounts. In M. Tonry (Ed.). *Crime and Justice: A Review of Research, 25*, 1–127.

Chazal, N. (2013). Beyond borders? The International Criminal Court and the Geopolitics of International Criminal Justice. *Griffith Law Review, 22*(3), 707–728.

Christie, N. (1977). Conflicts as property. *British Journal of Criminology, 17,* 1–19.

Clarke, D. C. (1991). Dispute resolution in China. *Journal of Chinese Law, 5,* 245–296.

Dinnen, S. (2003). *A kind of mending: Restorative justice in the Pacific Islands.* Canberra Pandanus.

Downes, D., & Nelken, D. (2011). Comparative criminology, globalization and the, Punitive Turn'. *Comparative Criminal Justice and Globalization, 27–47.*

Garland, D. (2001). *The culture of control* (Vol. 367). Oxford: Oxford University Press.

Garland, D. (2000, summer). The culture of high crime societies: Some preconditions of recent "Law and Order" policies. *British Journal of Criminology, 40*(3), 347–375.

Galvin, K. M. (2011). *Making connections: Readings in relational communication* (5th ed.). New York: Oxford University Press.

Gao, Q. B. (2003). *Research on Chinese customary law of ethnic minorities.* Beijing Tsinghua University.

Giffin, K., & Patton, B.R. (1971). *Fundamentals of interpersonal communication.* New York: Harper & Row.

Glaze, L. E., & Kaeble, D. (2013). BJS statisticians. *Correctional Populations in the United States.*

Golub, S. (2003). Non-State Justice Systems in Bangladesh and the Philippines: Paper prepared for the United Kingdom Department for International Development. http://gsdrc.org/docs/open/ds34.pdf

Haigh, Y. (2009). Desistance from crime: Reflections on the transitional experiences of young people with a history of offending. *Journal of Youth Studies, 12*(3), 307–322.

Haley, J. O. (1996). Crime prevention through restorative justice: Lessons from Japan. *Restorative Justice: International Perspectives, 349–372.*

Jiang, W. & Yang, R. (1990). *Introduction to People's Mediation.* China: Law Press.

Johnstone, G. (2013). *Restorative justice: Ideas, values, debates.* Routledge.

LaChappelle, L. (2014). Capital punishment in the era of globalization: A partial test of the marshall hypothesis among college students. *American Journal of Criminal Justice, 39*(4), 839–854.

Littlejohn, S. W., & Foss, K. A. (2008). *Theories of human communication* (8th ed.). Belmont, CA: Thomson Wadsworth.

Mann, R. M. (2014). Canada's Amended Youth Criminal Justice Act and the Problem of Serious Persistent Youth Offenders: Deterrence and the Globalization of Juvenile Justice. *JIJIS*, *14*, 59.

Mannozzi, G. (2002). From the "sword" to dialogue: towards a "dialectic" basis for penal mediation. In E. G. M. Weitekamp & H.-J. Kerner (Eds.), *Restorative Justice. Theoretical Foundations* (pp. 224–246). Cullompton: Willan.

Maxwell, G., & Hayes, H. (2007). Regional reviews, Section F, Pacific. In G. Johnstone & D. W. Van Ness (Eds.), *Handbook of Restorative Justice* (pp. 519–529). Cullompton: Willan.

Meyer, J., & O'Malley, P. (2005). Missing the punitive turn? Canadian criminal justice, "balance," and penal modernism. In J. Pratt, D. Brown, M. Brown, S. Hallsworth, & W. Morrison (Eds.), *The new punitiveness* (pp. 201–217). Devon, UK: Willan Publishing.

Moghadam, V. M. (2012). *Globalization and social movements: Islamism, feminism, and the global justice movement.* Rowman & Littlefield.

Morrison, B. (2005). Restorative justice in schools. In E. Elliott & R.M. Gordon (Eds.), *New directions in restorative justice* (pp. 26–52). Cullompton: Willan.

Muncie, J. (2011). On globalisation and exceptionalism. *Comparative Criminal Justice and Globalization*, 87–105.

Ota, T. (2003). Introduction: The development of victimology and victim support in Asia. *Victims and Criminal Justice: Asian Perspective*, 1–44.

Pratt, J. (2006). Beyond Evangelical Criminology: The Meaning and Significance of Restorative Justice. In I. Aertsen, T. Daems, & L. Robert (Eds.), *Institutionalizing Restorative Justice* (pp. 44–67). Cullompton, Devon: Willan.

Pruitt, D. G., & Kim, S. H. (2004). *Social conflict: Escalation, stalemate, and settlement* (3rd ed.). Boston: Mcgraw-Hill.

Skelton, A. (2007). Regional reviews: Africa. *Handbook of Restorative Justice*, 468–477.

Tauri, J. M. (2017). Indigenous peoples and the globalization of restorative justice. *Social Justice, 43*(3), 46–67.

Tauri, J. M. (2014). An Indigenous commentary on the globalisation of restorative justice. *British Journal of Community Justice, 12*(2), 35–55.

Thibaut, J., & Kelley, H. (1959). *The social psychology of groups.* New York: Wiley.

Tonry, M. (2006). Prospects for institutionalization of restorative justice initiatives in Western countries. In Ivo Aertsen, Tom Daems, & Luc Robert, (Eds.), *Institutionalizing Restorative Justice* (pp. 1–24). Portland: Willan.

Udombana, N. (2003). Globalization of Justice and the Special Court for Sierra Leone's War Crimes. *Emory Int'l L. Rev., 17*, 55.

United Nations. (1999). Rome Statute of the International Criminal Court. *Social Justice*, 125–143.

Urbina, M. G., & Álvarez, S. E. (2016). Neoliberalism, criminal justice and Latinos: The contours of neoliberal economic thought and policy on criminalization. *Latino Studies, 14*(1), 33–58.

Van Ness, D.W. (2007). North America. In G. Johnstone & D. W. Van Ness (Eds.), *Handbook of restorative justice* (pp. 510–519). Cullompton: Willan.

Wang, P., Di, X., & Wan, K.H. (2007). Asia. In G. Johnstone & D. W. Van Ness (Eds.) *Handbook of restorative justice* (pp. 477–488). Cullompton: Willan.

Wenzelburger, G. (2016). A global trend toward law and order harshness? *European Political Science Review*, *8*(4), 589–613.

Willemsens, J., & Walgrave, L. (2007). Europe. In G. Johnstone & D. W. Van Ness (Eds.), *Handbook of restorative justice* (pp. 488–499). Cullompton: Willan.

Wonders, N. A. (2016). Just-in-time justice: Globalization and the changing character of law, order, and power. *Critical Criminology*, *24*(2), 201–216.

Wright, M. (1991). *Justice for Victims and Offenders: A Restorative Response to Crime*. Milton Keynes: Open University Press.

Chapter 3

The Restorative Family

Restorative circles continue to be used in some cultures and communities to address conflicts in the family/tribe/community (Menkel-Meadow, 2014). As discussed earlier, these dispute resolution strategies anthropologically preceded the development of formalized legal systems and evoke procedural, emotional, and spiritual dimensions unconsidered by traditional Western jurisprudence (Boniface, 2012; Flies-Away & Garrow, 2013). Restorative practices in general seem to satisfy deeply human needs, which may be seen as both foundational and universal (Flies-Away & Garrow, 2013). The profoundly intimate nature of familial conflict, violence, wrongdoing, and strife make for an ideal venue to consider the value of adopting a communication perspective to better understand how restorative practices might work to improve relationships. Restorative practices connect with families at many stages, including premarital counseling, child welfare, and palliative/end-of-life care.

More profoundly than mere speculation, there are some empirical data points, which support the hypothesis of restorative forms of justice as foundational to the human experience. For example, children as young as three will retaliate to unfairness whether they themselves experience or witness it (Riedl, Jensen, Call, & Tomasello, 2015). Children in these experiments were keener to respond to the suffering of others than for any perceived need for retaliation or retribution. It seems the primary concern for these very young children is not who (if anyone) benefits from an act of injustice or how precisely the transgression occurred but rather the subjective experience of the victim. The victim could be the child herself, or a third party. Preschool-aged children do not appear to have a notion of justice based in deterrence or revenge (e.g., McCullough, Kurzban, & Tabak, 2013) but out of a concern for victim welfare and fairness (Riedl et al., 2015).

This chapter focuses on restorative practices in families from both proce-duralist and structuralist perspectives. Many programs and projects primarily operationalize family/parental engagement in a restorative process within the context of a school or as representatives of the community (Green, Willging, Zamarin, Dehaiman, & Ruiloba, 2019). In practice, there are many other ways families engage the practices of restoration beyond school-based restorative justice. Researchers have been led to consider which of these contexts affect each member within that family system (Beck, Britto, & Andrews, 2007).

To examine restorative justice and the family seems to require considering the places and groups individuals find themselves connected and embedded. A family member (or unit) does not stand alone. A parent may be the victim of bullying at work. Children may have experienced restorative discipline in their school. Elders may have been part of a talking circle as a member of their church. Additionally, there seems little end to the traumas that indi-vidual family members may have experienced or have perpetrated on one another, which may lead them to an experience with restorative processes such as in the case of substance abuse, child or parental neglect, lack of edu-cation, mental health issues, caregiving responsibilities, family disarray and distress, and inequality (Beck et al., 2007). Rarely, it seems, in restorative processes, is anything cut and dry.

RESTORATIVE FAMILIES AND
RELIGIOUS COMMUNITIES

Restorative principles have the potential, it seems, to connect with many stages of an individual's and a family's life. As in instances of child welfare and family violence, restorative practices simultaneously appeal to the fun-damental humanity of the offender while demanding she, he, or they take responsibility for, her, or their criminal acts. Sullivan and Tifft (2001) caution that such a balancing act must be performed unsanctimoniously. To that end, they forefront the historical, cultural, and practical role of religious com-munities in the lives of families engaging in restorative practices. However, the powerful role of religious communities in the cultural lives of many Americans should not be overlooked.

Historically, there was very little contribution from theologians in the then-emerging European positivist criminology of the 1800s. Rather, Christian theologians proved resistant to comment upon or to connect their own faith and faith communities to any dialogue around the subject of justice policy. Culture seemed to be barreling through post-Enlightenment empiricism and rationality as the basis for the etiology of criminal behavior (Sarre, 1999). Faith was, in such a world, unnecessary to explain the causes for antisocial criminal conduct. Western justice practices were then generally considered retributive. Allard and Northey (2001) identify this as a strange element of early Christian conceptions of justice.

A surprising connection between faith and families impacted by crime came, then, not with the prevention or explanation of crime, but with the question of how communities, families, and individuals would respond to criminal acts and the perpetrators of those acts. Quakers and Puritans began to focus on the theological rationale for the dedicated rehabilitation of criminals (Sherman, 2001). A more robust and informed modern debate concerning the interaction of faith and crime followed.

Criminological focus on restorative practices in the 1970s brought about a renewed dialog around these subjects in faith communities. For the first time, questions were being explored, which linked postmodern criminology with liberation theology. The proponents of each found they shared much common ground (Forrester, 1997). In the intervening forty years, many religious scholars and practitioners have now firmly embraced restorative justice principles, practices, and values (Friedrichs, 2006; Sullivan & Tifft, 2001). Criminological and faith communities, once separated by a mutual lack of concern or interest, find value in their mutual connection: families (Hadley, 2001; 2006; Richards, 2009; Burnside, 2007). In some circles, faith-based justice is all but indistinguishable from restorative justice (Richards, 2009; Sarre & Young, 2011). Christian restorative justice programs have been known to support social policy initiatives such as improved education, fair employment, safe housing, and criminal justice reform (Hadley, 2006).

This connection extends beyond the more Western, Judeo-Christian culture, most common to many communities within the United States. Other studies have connected restorative practices with teachings from Taoist, Buddhist, and Confucian traditions, the Code of Lipit-Ishtar (1875 BCE), and the Code of Hammurabi (1700 BCE) (Richards, 2009), first-nations courts (Sullivan & Tifft, 2001), Pacific Islander cosmological/theological systems (Maxwell & Hayes, 2006), and the Afghani *jirga* (Zehr, 2002, p. 62). While some of these practices bear only a passing relationship with restorative justice, there remains a wide diversity of contemporary restorative justice options available to families in crisis (Dignan, 2005; Richards, 2009).

Critically, this postmodern reimagining and rebranding of Christian theology as fully restorative with a deep, abiding concern with justice should not mask behaviors of some espoused members of these faith communities, which all too frequently appear more as selective vengeance with sanctioned retribution. Take, for example, the typical response to the myriad church/pastoral sex abuse cases, handled through the courts, leading to an almost laser-like attention on financial compensation rather than emotional healing or psychological restoration (Gavrielides & Coker, 2005). This kind of response is far from aligned with restorative values or practices. "It is not at all unusual to hear a Christian minister decry the rising tide of crime and immorality in print or in the pulpit, but it is rare indeed to hear a Christian minister exhorting the faithful to actually dare to love their enemies" (McHugh, 1978, p. 133). Instead, a truly restorative response from Christian faith communities in America has been, and continues to be, rare. Were Christian communities more willing to adopt a restorative communicative perspective in the wake of conflict, their responses could focus on the relationships between their members, highlight the belonging to the community, and evolve responses to reintegrate the offenders. Such a response has been modeled.

In 2006, a gunman attacked an Amish community school, killing six young girls in the process. The community responded not with calls for judgment or for a desire to get even. Neither did they attempt to merely move on with their own grief, ignoring the attacker through the ensuing legal process. Rather, the Amish community members, intimately linked webs of family relationships, reached out to the attacker's own wife and family with offers of kindness, sorrow, compassion, empathy, and even material support (Kraybill, Nolt, & Weaver-Zercher, 2010). The response was so radically at odds with the dominant cultural notion of what is appropriate in terms of a response to violence, crime, and violation, some perceived it as verging on injustice toward those victimized and traumatized by the gunman's actions (Gottlieb, 2006). In this case, the Amish community's response demonstrated the possibility of a restorative alternative as a means of balancing a moral inequity (Brunk, 2001).

Family is often defined in relational terms, communicatively connoting ingroup and outgroup membership, rights, and responsibilities. The oft-cited restorative African concept of *ubuntu* seems most appropriate. Boniface (2012), focusing in mediation-centric African family-law, defines *ubuntu* as it as a "human being is a human being through other human beings" or "'I am because you are' or 'I exist because you exist'" (103). For family members in this context, mediation becomes a method of developing moral character among participants, not a process of compromise or settlement (Daicoff, 2015). The often intimate interconnectivity of a family unit, the potential harm that can occur in such close relationships, as well as the numerous contexts in which families find themselves interacting (e.g., home, school, places of worship) make the opportunities for restorative processes "a better kind of justice" (Jeong, McGarrell & Hipple, 2012, p. 372). These contexts are particularly strong in their power to communicate belonging, identity, and relational inclusion.

FAMILY AS "COMMUNITY"

Both restorative justice theory and the theory of reintegrative shaming (Braithwaite, 1989) posit a triumvirate of participants in restorative processes: victim, offender, and community. The "community" component takes on a variety of forms depending on the restorative process and program (see chapter 5). Sometimes, the community is represented by a circle of peers, tribal elders, a mediator or pair of co-mediators, or classmates. Circle process, especially in cases of nontraditional family structure, have been found to "reduce anxiety, slow down the participants' interactions, reduce hostility, create a community within the participants, communicate mutual respect for all present, and unify them in common values and goals" (Daicoff, 2015, p. 436). Family members or a family unit can become the "community" the restorative process needs, at other times perhaps taking on a supportive or victim role. Nowhere is this truer than when a family opts to develop a restorative form of discipline.

Restorative justice theory has been recently linked with parental discipline, specifically positive parental discipline, which highlights reasoning and empathetic concern for victims (Patrick & Gibbs, 2012). When the family operates as a community which adopts restorative discipline, it foregrounds the values of accountability, relational repair, nonviolence, negative association with aggression, harm repair, and destigmatization of the offender (Ahmed & Braithwaite, 2006; Harris, 2001). Restorative discipline in families helps to develop reflective skills in children, allowing them to better practice empathy, caring, and comforting (Lai, Siu, & Shek, 2015).

These affective skills, practices, and philosophies of discipline do not remain within the family unit, but rather, transfer beyond it. It has been found that families that adopt restorative discipline, foster a positive (rather than punitive) climate, and offer parental support lead their adolescent children to more robustly develop their own moral emotional capacity (Valdés-Cuervo, Alcántar-Nieblas, Martínez-Ferrer, & Parra-Pérez, 2018). Children steeped in restorative discipline are more likely to defend victims when they witness bullying. This particular finding is significant as previous research (see Carlo, McGinley, Hayes, Batenhorst, & Wilkinson, 2007) has shown parental discipline had no effect on altruistic behavior when the child could face retaliation from a bully. It seems restorative discipline helps develop both moral responsibility and prosocial behaviors in adolescents to the point where they will intercede between victim and bully in an effort to right the moral wrong of which they are witness.

Family Courts

In the context of contemporary American family courts, restorative circle processes provide a method of conflict response that is more holistic and therapeutic than more traditional, adversarial processes (Daicoff, 2015). The use of restorative circles in family law is part of a broader movement within the legal profession toward a more comprehensive response to practical and legal questions such as how best to heal and repair the relationships of those involved. Restorative values of inclusion, respect, autonomy, and agency are particularly relevant in family law cases. Circle process broadens the spectrum of participants, bringing more individuals to the table, often literally.

For practitioners of family law, a number of factors make restorative circles appealing. First, the goal is to establish a safe, inclusive context where family members can participate, provide information, offer solutions, compromise, and support one another. They are more likely to have greater investment in maintaining whatever agreements they negotiate, as well (Daicoff, 2015). Next, restorative circle values (e.g., respect, equality, pride, toleration, collaboration) aim to promote better post-dispute family relationships and communication. Finally, circle processes seek to grow a family to self-police in order to avoid future litigation. By these three goals, restorative circles emphasize participant (rather than mediator or judicial) responsibility in keeping agreements viable.

This begs the question of how circle processes come into contact with family courts. Often established within or beneath a punitive framework, restorative programs tend to operate alongside traditional family courts. Participants can thus have the option of restorative processes with the ever-constant threat of a more formal, legalistic process waiting in the wings. In these cases, families may have both a restorative and a retributive system available for them. In contrast to this "both and" approach advocated by McNevin (2010), other research claims restorative approaches will be more effective when they are viewed in contrast to a traditional court process. Restorative programs might be better off setting themselves apart from, rather than as a part of the court system (Jeong, McGarrell, & Hipple 2012). When comparing restorative, Family Groups Conferencing (FGCs), and retributive approaches in family courts, results are generally in agreement.

Luke and Lind (2002) found FGCs could reduce re-offending for first time young offenders up to 20 percent. Similarly, McGarrell and Hipple (2007) found FGC participants less likely to re-offend (within two years) compared to a control group. When FGC participants re-offend, it was at a lower frequency, as well. The biggest changes in recidivism among FGC participants are seen with younger juveniles, girls, and for those who commit serious crimes with personal victims (Armour, Windsor, Aguilar, and Taub,

2008; de Beus and Rodriguez, 2007; Rodriguez, 2007). Some research claims FGCs lead to increased perspective-taking and empathetic concern, as well (Sherman & Strang, 2007).

Notably, when outcomes have been studied over an even longer (twelve-year) period, no statistically significant differences were found between participants in an FGC and control group participants in terms of prevalence for reoffending (Jeong, McGarrell, & Hipple 2012). Braithwaite (2002), perhaps more prescient than given credit for, anticipated these results. Practitioners were cautioned that FGCs should not be developed into or used as a one-time intervention. Rather, they ought to be considered as interventions repeated over time and community-integrated in order to have maximum impact in assisting family members develop their understanding of their role in community and their moral obligation to those communities. One such approach that rarely operates as a one-time intervention is a restorative method of counseling.

Restorative Approach Counseling

Families in distress or those facing challenges they feel unequipped to address may seek out counseling. This might occur at any stage in the family life cycle from early relationship or pre-marital counseling, following a trauma, or as family members look to the care and comfort of aging loved ones. Restorative Approach (RA) counseling is a method of family counseling in which the relational and communicative systems linking all family members is the focus. Like other restorative practices, Restorative approach "is an ethos and practice built on the hypothesis that addressing harms and challenges within communities or between individuals is best achieved by building or restoring relationships" (Williams, Reed, Rees, & Segrott, 2018, p. 171). RA is premised on the same communicative perspective, which identifies intra-group message-exchange as constitutive of family identity and belonging.

Chronologically, the first stage of family life wherein restorative approach counseling might find value is in premarital counseling (Borton, 2018). Participation in some form of prenuptial education is common (Silliman, 2003). The programs often employ psychological metric evaluation and discussion with a professional counselor or clergy member (Madison & Madison, 2013). In such cases, the community of concern might extend to include not only the couple entering marriage but also their respective faith communities, children, and extended families, which may be less than fully restorative in their values and practices. As we've noted, according to some restorative theorists and practitioners, restorative justice cannot occur in the absence of community, with diminished returns for communities of unequal power dynamics (Johnstone, 2002; Pranis, 1998). Thus far, it seems there is little extant research (longitudinal or otherwise) on premarital counseling programs' effectiveness and even less so on the coordination of these programs with a restorative philosophy (Stanley, Blumberg, & Markman, 1999). Following the typically optimistic and forward-looking premarital stage in a family's development, comes what is often a more routine and mundane domestic existence.

Sadly, times of crisis, pain, violence, and loss also face many family groups. It is at this stage in which the tenets and practices of restorative justice find significant purchase. Restorative practices have been used to address significant issues, such as domestic violence. As the name implies, in family group counseling a family system's membership comes together in order to discuss issues of concern relating to the family, especially the children (Sen, Morris, Burford, Featherstone, & Webb, 2018).

Often domestic violence situations are the point of entry for child protective services, formal legal intervention, and engagement with social services. Family group conferences are sometimes explicitly barred in cases of domestic violence (Ptacek, 2010). Sen and colleagues (2018) critique this unilateral exclusion of restorative practices in the cases of domestic violence. They question contemporary separation policies (wherein a woman's separation from a male offender is viewed as the only workable choice, is state-mandated, and is done to her regardless of her preferences or circumstances). In reality, many male offenders continue to have contact with the victims and witnesses to domestic abuse, their children. Critics of the use of restorative practices in family violence cases have identified three key issues: victim safety, perpetrator accountability, and foregrounding victim needs and experiences (Ptacek, 2010). There seems, however, to be potential for at least partly restorative responses and opportunities in some cases of domestic violence.

Family group conferences offer a child welfare service and domestic violence response, which is both more humane and effective (Mason, Ferguson, Morris, Munton, & Sen, 2017; Stanley & Humphreys, 2017). Mediation might occur between victim and offender; willing parties could plan for the security and welfare of the family's children. In the United States, domestic violence separation policies and the ensuing removal, detention, and incarceration of the male offenders disproportionately affects marginalized communities. This includes the poor, non-white, refugee, immigrant, and LGBT+ communities (Coker & Macquoid, 2015). Those communities are the same that experience disproportionate surveillance, policing, and incarceration feeding inequity, economic insecurity, and community disruption (Sen et al., 2018). This cycle creates communities in which domestic violence remains far more likely (Coker & Macquoid, 2015).

Restorative processes, including family group conferencing, have the potential to address another critique of current social service programs. According to Hester (2011), domestic violence programs frequently face critiques for their siloed approach, focusing on women *or* children *or* the men involved. This leaves very little space for restorative, family-based approaches. Research finds most conferences, which occur in siloed programs based on separation tend to be pragmatic (focusing on child protection and excluding male perpetrators), and are rarely restorative (which are premised on the desired inclusion of paternal and maternal networks) (Sen et al., 2018).

When restorative practices are used in cases where domestic abuse is present, they have a particular ethos and focus. They focus on intimate engagement with male offenders and their family networks to talk about what occurred, and how each family system member can help develop ways to mitigate future pains. Rather than mandatory exclusion, there is community reintegration (Braithwaite, 1989).

The potential for inclusive, malleable, and progressive restorative approach counseling and family group conferencing used in cases of domestic violence is significant. For recalcitrant offenders, admitting culpability, voluntarily participating, and committing to real change, this is an opportunity to recognize the real role they often continue to play in the lives of their children. As always, victim safety and potential re-victimization should never be far from consideration. Restorative practices more fully recognize the diversity of victim populations, the humanity of offenders, and the need for strong, robust, and connected communities.

Restorative processes ask for active, engaged participation from not only offenders, but from victims, as well. McNevin (2010) offers a "both and" position for restorative approach counseling and family separation policies. Ultimately, there is a therapeutic imperative in both family counseling literature and practice, which prioritizes forgiveness on the victim's behalf as a goal (James, 2010). All of the traditional cautions against both forced apology and forgiveness-seeking apply in these, and other, sensitive domestic cases. More restorative options might be offered alongside therapeutic work, not as a replacement, but as an additional practice highlighting responsibility and support for both victims and offenders (McNevin, 2010). Even if never put into practice, restorative practices have much to offer family counseling for consideration regarding dominant discourse, social systems, and structural patterns of inequality and power (Dallos & Urry, 1999). Restorative counseling from a communication perspective would likely generate a variety of different outcomes than traditional, cookie-cutter reactions to domestic violence.

Specifically, some of these key considerations in cases of child welfare include assessing what the child is worried most about, what in their situation is working well, and what must happen regarding the identified worries (Lehmann, Jordan, Bolton, Huynh, & Chigbu, 2012). Responses from each contributing member of a family system (including perpetrators of violence) would seem to be beneficial in both understanding and preventing harm. Restorative family counseling is, like other restorative justice-based programs, a movement toward purposeful engagement with all appropriate offenders, and a move away from punitive actions and philosophies. It is part of restorative justice's cooperative philosophy to engage all stakeholders. Restorative interventions are neither paternalistic nor adversarial. They use strengths-based language and focus on relationship-building rather than relationship deficits and maladaptive behaviors (Lehmann et al., 2012). Thus, counselors and practitioners include the family system itself (as fully as is safely possible) into a restorative experience where they develop the proactive skills as they co-create their own way healthily forward. Restoration, in these cases, is a means to moral, familial, and community growth.

End of Life Decision-Making

While certainly there are individuals who neither marry nor have children, and thankfully even fewer become victims of domestic violence, aging and death are a certainty. Here too, then, it could be valuable to consider what restorative justice theory might offer to perhaps the ultimate question of our mortality, community, and agency. How does adopting a communicative perspective constitute a new perspective on palliative and end-of-life care?

No doubt inflammatory public discourse, controversy, and impassioned views have always existed around death. Perhaps a restorative reconsideration of the subjects of euthanasia and assisted suicide would at least provide a novel perspective to sidestep some seemingly ancient arguments. Let us hypothesize a scenario in which an elderly, terminally ill parent wishes to end their own life and asks for a family member's help in performing the act.

As it stands, current prohibitions against euthanasia and assisted suicide would likely polarize and separate the relational intimates. The state nonconsensually casts the deceased as a victim; the assistant is the accused, the offender, or the defendant (Llewellyn, 2012). If the relationship between the deceased and the assistant were, however, reconsidered as one of equality, whose agency and freedom was respected it could "lead to more effective and compassionate responses to cases of euthanasia and assisted suicide" (Valdés-Cuervo et al., 2018, p. 157). Such a response requires a fundamental reorientation to understanding harm in these cases. Such a practice would reorient restorative theory as a proactive and preventative activity, involving the relevant family and community members, with each constituency sequentially considered in their victimhood. Such a re-imagining might allow a more nuanced and complex understanding of what happened and what is about to happen. Proactive restorative processes might then be engaged in a more democratic, robust, and inclusive process.

From the dining room table to the counselor's office to the sanctuary, family members encounter restorative processes in a variety of ways. Some contexts seem to offer opportunities for parents to engage children in more helpful disciplinary practices. Some offer social workers and counselors new perspectives on the necessary response to transgressions within the family. Finally, still others touch the knowledge of our own mortality. By stretching the bounds of what can be included under the umbrella of restorative practices (i.e., by working from a structuralist perspective of restorative justice), we do not dilute its power, but rather, extend the influence of its generally beneficial outcomes.

REFERENCES

Ahmed, E., & Braithwaite, V. (2006). Forgiveness, reconciliation, and shame: Three key variables in reducing school bullying. *Journal of Social Issues, 62*(2), 347–370. https:// doi.org/10.1111/j.1540-4560.2006.00454.x.

Allard, P., & Northey, W. (2001). Christianity: The rediscovered roots of restorative justice. In M. L. Hadley (Ed.), *The spiritual roots of restorative justice* (pp. 119–142). SUNY Press.

Armour, M. P., Windsor, L. C., Aguilar, J., & Taub, C. (2008). A pilot study of a faith-based restorative justice intervention for Christian and non-Christian offenders. *Journal of Psychology and Christianity, 27*(2), 159–167.

Beck, E., Britto, S., & Andrews, A. (2007). *In the shadow of death: Restorative justice and death row families.* Oxford University Press.

Boniface, A. E. (2012). African-style mediation and Western-style divorce and family mediation: Reflections for the South African context. *Potchefstroom Electronic Law Journal/Potchefstroomse Elektroniese Regsblad, 15*(5). https://doi.org/10 .4314/pelj.v15i5.10.

Borton, I.M. (2018). Transforming marital conflict through restorative justice. In P. M. Kellett & T. G. Matyók (Eds.), *Transforming conflict through communication in personal, family, and working relationships* (pp. 131–144). Rowman & Littlefield.

Braithwaite, J. (2002). *Restorative justice and responsive regulation.* Oxford University Press.

Braithwaite, J. (1989). *Crime, shame and reintegration.* Cambridge University Press.

Brunk, C. (2001). Restorative justice and the philosophical theories of criminal punishment. In M. L. Hadley (Ed.), *The spiritual roots of restorative justice* (pp. 31–56). SUNY Press.

Burnside, J. (2007). Retribution and restoration in Biblical texts. In G. Johnstone & D. W. Van Ness (Eds.), *Handbook of restorative justice* (pp. 132–148). Willan.

Carlo, G., McGinley, M., Hayes, R., Batenhorst, C., & Wilkinson, J. (2007). Parenting styles or practices? Parenting, sympathy, and prosocial behavior among adolescents. *The Journal of Genetic Psychology: Research, Theory on Human Development, 168*(2), 147–176. https://doi.org/10.3200/GNTP.168.2.

Coker, D., & Macquoid, A. (2015). Why opposing hyper-incarceration should be central to the work of the anti-domestic violence movement. *University of Miami Race & Social Justice Law Review, 585*(8). https://papers.ssrn.com/sol3/papers.cfm?abstract_id=2638902.

Daicoff, S. S. (2015). Families in circle process: Restorative justice in family law. *Family Court Review, 53*(3), 427–438. https://doi.org/10.1111/fcre.12164.

Dallos, R., & Urry, A. (1999). Abandoning our parents and grandparents: Does social construction mean the end of systemic family therapy. *Journal of Family Therapy, 21*(2), 161–186. https://doi.org/10.1111/1467-6427.00112.

de Beus, K., & Rodriguez, N. (2007). Restorative justice practice: An examination of program completion and recidivism. *Journal of Criminal Justice, 35*(3), 337–347 https://doi.org/10.1016/j.crimjus.2007.03.009.

Dignan, J. (2004). *Understanding victims and restorative justice.* McGraw-Hill Education.

Flies-Away, J. T., & Garrow, C. E. (2013). Healing to wellness courts: Therapeutic jurisprudence. *Michigan State Law Review*, 403–450. https://heinonline.org/HOL/P?h=hein.journals/mslr2013&i=425.

Forrester, D. B. (1997). *Christian justice and public policy* (Vol. 10). Cambridge University Press.

Friedrichs, D.O. (2006). Restorative justice and the criminological enterprise. In D. Sullivan & L. Tifft (Eds.), *The handbook of restorative justice: A global perspective* (pp. 439–451). Routledge.

Gavrielides, T., & Coker, D. (2005). Restoring faith: Resolving the Roman Catholic Church's sexual scandals through restorative justice (Working Paper I). *Contemporary Justice Review, 8*(4), 345–365. https://doi.org/10.1080/1028258050 0334205.

Gottlieb, D. (2006). Not always divine. Retrieved October 17, 2018. http://www.cross-currents.com/archives/2006/10/17/not-always-divine/.

Hadley, M.L. (Ed.). (2001). *The spiritual roots of restorative justice.* SUNY Press.

Hadley, M.L. (2006). Spiritual foundations of restorative justice. In D. Sullivan & L. Tifft (Eds.), *The handbook of restorative justice: A global perspective* (pp. 174–187). Routledge.

Harris, N. (2001). Shaming and shame: Regulations drink-driving. In E. Ahmed, N. Harris, J. Braithwaite, & V. Braithwaite (Eds.), *Shame management through reintegration* (pp. 73–210). Cambridge University.

Hester, M. (2011). The three planet model: Towards an understanding of contradictions in approaches to women and children's safety in contexts of domestic violence. *British Journal of Social Work, 41*(5), 837–853. https://doi.org/10.1093/bjsw/bcr095.

James K. (2007). The interactional process of forgiveness and responsibility: A critical assessment of the family therapy literature. In C. Flaskas, I. McCarthy & J. Sheehan (Eds.), *Hope and despair in narrative and family therapy: Adversity, forgiveness and reconciliation.* Routledge.

Jeong, S., McGarrell, E. F., & Hipple, N. K. (2012). Long-term impact of family group conferences on re-offending: The Indianapolis restorative justice experiment. *Journal of Experimental Criminology, 8*(4), 369–385. https://doi.org/10.1 007/s11292-012-9158-8.

Johnstone, G. (2002). *Restorative Justice: Ideas, Values, Debates.* Portland, OR: Willan.

Koss M., Bachar K., & Hopkins C. (2006). Disposition and treatment of Juvenile Sex Offenders from the perspective of restorative justice. In H. Barbaree & W. Marshall (Eds.), *The juvenile sex offender* (2nd ed., pp. 336–357). The Guildford Press.

Kraybill, D. B., Nolt, S. M., & Weaver-Zercher, D. L. (2010). *Amish grace: How forgiveness transcended tragedy.* John Wiley & Sons.

Lai, F. H., Siu, A. M. H., & Shek, D. T. L. (2015). Individual and social predictors of prosocial behavior among Chinese adolescents in Hong Kong. *Frontier in Pediatrics, 3*, 1–8. https://doi.org/10.3389/fped.2015.00039.

Lehmann, P., Jordan, C., Bolton, K. W., Huynh, L., & Chigbu, K. (2012). Solution-focused brief therapy and criminal offending: A family conference tool for work in restorative justice. *Journal of Systemic Therapies, 31*(4), 49–62. https://doi.org /10.1521/jsyt.2012.31.4.49.

Llewellyn, J. (2012). Restorative justice: Thinking relationally about justice. In J. Downie & J. J. Llewellyn (Eds.), *Being relational: Reflections on relational theory and health law* (pp. 89–108). UBC Press.

Luke, G., & Lind, B. (2002). *Reducing juvenile crime: Conferencing versus court.* New South Wales Bureau of Crime Statistics and Research. https://www.ncjrs.gov /App/Publications/abstract.aspx?ID=194918.

Madison, J. K., & Madison. L.S. (2013). A review of research-based interventions on marriage preparation. *Journal of Rational-Emotional Cognitive-Behavioral Therapy, 31*, 67–74. https://doi.org/10.1007/s10942-013-0160-5.

Mason, P., Ferguson, H., Morris, K., Monton, T., & Sen, R. (2017). Leeds Family Valued. Evaluation report, July 2017. http://dera.ioe.ac.uk/id/eprint/29566.

Maxwell, G., & Hayes, H. (2006). Restorative justice developments in the Pacific region: A comprehensive survey. *Contemporary Justice Review, 9*(2), 127–154. https://doi.org/10.1080/10282580600784929.

McCullough, M. E., Kurzban, R., & Tabak, B. A. (2013). Cognitive systems for revenge and forgiveness. *Behavioral and Brain Sciences, 36*(1), 1–15. https://doi .org/10.1017/S140525X11002160.

McGarrell, E., & Hipple, N. K. (2007). Family group conferencing and re-offending among first-time juvenile offenders: The Indianapolis experiment. *Justice Quarterly, 24*(2), 221–246. https://doi.org/10.1080/07418820701294789.

McHugh, G. A. (1978). *Christian faith and criminal justice: Toward a Christian response to crime and punishment.* Paulist Press.

McNevin, E. (2010). Applied restorative justice as a complement to systemic family therapy: Theory and practice implications for families experiencing intra-familial adolescent sibling incest. *Australian and New Zealand Journal of Family Therapy, 31*(1), 60–72. https://doi.org/10.1375/anft.31.1.60.

Menkel-Meadow, C. (2014). Unsettling the lawyers: Other forms of justice in Indigenous claims of expropriation, abuse, and injustice. *University of Toronto Law Journal, 64*(4), 620–639. https://doi.org/10.3138/utlj.2418.

Patrick, R. B., & Gibbs, J. C. (2012). Inductive discipline, parental expression of disappointed expectation, and moral identity in adolescence. *Journal of Youth Adolescence, 41*(8), 973–983. https://doi.org/10.1007/s10964-9698-7.

Pranis, K. (1998). Building Community Support for Restorative Justice: Principles and Strategies. Justice Orientation Training Information Package. Restorative Justice and Dispute Resolution Branch. Correctional Services. Canada.

Ptacek, J. (2010). Resisting co-optation: Three feminist challenges to antiviolence work. In J. Ptacek (Ed.), *Interpersonal violence. Restorative justice violence against women* (pp. 5–36). Oxford University Press.

Richards, K. (2009). Rewriting and Reclaiming History: An analysis of the emergence of restorative justice in western criminal systems. *International Journal of Restorative Justice, 5*(1), 104–128.

Riedl, K., Jensen, K., Call, J., & Tomasello, M. (2015). Restorative justice in children. *Current Biology, 25*(13), 1731–1735. https://doi.org/10.1016/j.cub.2015.05.014.

Rodriguez, N. (2007). Restorative justice at work: Examining the impact of restorative justice resolutions on juvenile recidivism. *Crime and Delinquency, 53*(3), 355–379 https://doi.org/10.1177/0011128705285983.

Sarre, R. (1999). Restorative justice: Translating the theory into practice. *University of Notre Dame Australian Law Review, 1*(1), 11–26. https://heinonline.org/HOL/P?h=hein.journals/undauslr1&i=17.

Sarre, R., & Young, J. (2011). Christian approaches to the restorative justice movement: Observations on scripture and praxis. *Contemporary Justice Review, 14*(3), 345–355. https://doi.org/10.1080/10282580.2011.589670.

Sen, R., Morris, K., Burford, G., Featherstone, B., & Webb, C. (2018). "When you're sitting in the room with two people one of whom . . . has bashed the hell out of the other": Possibilities and challenges in the use of FGCs and restorative approaches following domestic violence. *Children and Youth Services Review, 88*, 441–449. https://doi.org/10.1016/j.childyouth.2018.03.027.

Sherman, L. (2001). Two protestant ethics and the spirit of restoration. In H. Strang & J. Braithwaite (Eds.), *Restorative justice and civil society* (pp. 35–55). Cambridge University Press.

Sherman, L. W., & Strang, H. (2007). *Restorative justice: The evidence*. Smith Institute.

Silliman, B. (2003). Building healthy marriages through early and extended outreach with youth." *Journal of Psychology and Theology, 31*(3), 270–282. https://doi.org/10.1177/009164710303100311.

Stanley, S. M., Blumberg, S. L., & Markman, H. J. (1999). Helping couples fight for their marriages: The PREP approach. In R. Berger & M. T. Hannah (Eds.), *Preventive approaches in couples therapy* (pp. 279–303). Taylor & Francis.

Stanley, N., & Humphreys, C. (2017). Identifying the key components of a "whole family" intervention for families experiencing domestic violence and abuse.

Journal of Gender-Based Violence, *1*(1), 99–115. https://doi.org/10.1332/239868
017X14913081639164.

Sullivan, D., & Tifft, L. (2001). *Restorative justice: Healing the foundations of our
everyday lives*. Willow Tree Press.

Valdés-Cuervo, A. A., Alcántar-Nieblas, C., Martínez-Ferrer, B., & Parra-Pérez, L.
(2018). Relations between restorative parental discipline, family climate, parental
support, empathy, shame, and defenders in bullying. *Children and Youth Services
Review*, *95*, 152–159. https://doi.org/10.1016/j.childyouth.2018.10.015.

Williams, A., Reed, H., Rees, G., & Segrott, J. (2018). Improving relationship–based
practice, practitioner confidence and family engagement skills through restorative
approach training. *Children and Youth Services Review, 93*, 170–177. https://doi
.org/10.1016/j.childyouth.2018.07.014.

Zehr, H. (2002). *The little book of restorative justice*. Good Books.

Chapter 4

Restorative Justice in American Schools

THE AMERICAN SCHOOL

As in most schools in the Western, English-speaking world, the majority of the history of discipline in American schools can best be summarized as "misbehave, get hit." The tradition of viewing schoolteachers *in loco parentis*, as surrogate parents, afforded teachers significant leniency to dole out punishment and reward as they saw fit. For most of American school history, discipline mainly consisted of corporal punishment with perhaps a cane, paddle, strap, switch, or yardstick. While the vast majority of American schools have moved away from corporal punishment, it remains legal in a number of U.S. states in public schools, as well as legal in private schools in almost every state.

Beyond corporal punishment, the turn to less violent forms of discipline has not been without its criticisms, most notably of disproportionate and differential treatment of minority students (particularly African American boys) and those of lower socioeconomic means (Drakeford, 2006; Fabelo et al., 2011; McKown & Weinstein, 2002; U.S. Department of Justice, 2014). The stigma and stereotypes of overly aggressive behavior marks many minority youth (Rudd, 2016). Seeking to understand the reasons for these disparities in treatment, implicit bias has been suggested as one possible explanatory factor. Additionally, accounting for the unequal treatment of different groups of students seems to show teachers' subjective assessments of student behavior (Skiba, Michael, Nardo, & Peterson, 2002). While a middle-class white student is more likely to receive a modest disciplinary response such as a verbal reprimand, the data indicate that a lower-class African American student is significantly more likely to report receiving a more severe consequence, as captured by Fabelo et al.'s (2011) report on disproportionate discipline

in Texas schools. While accountability is necessary, it is too often disproportionately problematic and unequal (Fabelo et al., 2011). We next turn to
examine more deeply the school system as a particular context for restorative
work via a review of the practices of zero-tolerance discipline and its accompanying (and now cliché) schools-to-prison pipeline.

FAILURES AND FAULTS OF PUNITIVE SYSTEMS AND ZERO-TOLERANCE POLICIES

If not the first argument that comes to mind, the racial disproportionality
present in both our criminal justice and our school disciplinary systems
should be warrant enough to consider how more restorative practices might
be employed to more equitably address anti-social behaviors, especially in
the young. In the era of Black Lives Matter, and in the long American history of injustice, discrimination, and prejudice especially toward African-
American males, it is high time we examine "how and why students of color
are disproportionately punished in schools and overrepresented in the criminal justice system" (Wadhwa, 2013, p. 32). The racial caste system borne
from slavery, and perpetuated in Jim Crow laws, persists today in the US
penal system, where African American men are locked-up at a rate six times
that of white men (Alexander, 2010; Human Rights Watch, 2009). Cavanagh
(2009) insists those who work in the field of restorative practices in education have an ethical obligation to acknowledge that such work is intimately
linked to the punishments and consequences that disproportionately affect
minority students.

Beyond the long history of institutionalized racism in America, there are
additional, systemic factors that exacerbate these issues in major metropoli-
tan school districts. City schools are in a seemingly constant state of flux as
exemplified by the sometimes drastic, dramatic, and frequent leadership
changes and high staff attrition rates. Factors such as these have made embedding restorative practices into the fabric of schools additionally challenging
(Das, 2017).

Perhaps the most culpable program of failing students in terms of their
holistic inclusion and emotional development (twin hallmarks of restorative practices) is the set of draconian behavioral standards often dubbed
"zero tolerance." Flourishing in the final years of the twentieth century,
zero tolerance can be defined as a philosophy of action focusing school
disciplinary policies and practices on punishment, deterrence, and incapacitation (González, 2012). It has been long understood that "current
punitive conflict management approaches in schools tend to be ineffective
and disproportionately harmful to marginalized students" (Barnes, 2015,

p. ii). Broadly, zero tolerance is ineffective in achieving its disciplinary goals and is waning in its popularity (Advancement Project, 2010; APA, 2008; Fabelo et al., 2011; Mann, 2016). Zero tolerance policies frequently find themselves at odds with current democratic, student empowerment and engagement models (Anfara, Evans, & Lester, 2013). It is also a philosophy almost diametrically opposed to a philosophy of restoration, which would instead foreground inclusion, participant identity support, community belonging, and reintegration.

Add to this mix of poverty, profiling, and punishment other systemic realities, and the result is students excluded from their school communities at disproportionately high rates. They experience decreased academic achievement, school apathy, and failure to persist (González, 2012).

The school-to-prison pipeline is strengthened when a shaky student is expelled or suspended for misbehavior (Smith, 2015). Those who are suspended are often the least literate, and these educational deficits continue into the prison system. Upward of 70 percent of the incarcerated in 1997 had never graduated high school and a similar percent of juvenile offenders have learning disabilities. One-third of juvenile offenders read below the fourth-grade level (Wald & Losen, 2003). It's not surprising that the effort to reform our criminal justice system oftentimes begins in our school systems. "Today, there are schools across the country partaking in a larger social justice movement that includes proponents of restorative justice who are aiming to overhaul both the prison system and the punitive practices in schools" (Wadhwa, 2013, p. 44). This shift has the potential to reshape the current school discipline paradigm of how schools are run, students are treated, and problems addressed.

Current failures of "typical school discipline models are the result of their inability to turn disciplinary violations into learning experiences" (Suvall, 2009, p. 547). And while the first documented use of restorative justice in an educational setting began nearly thirty years ago, there ought to be caution to the notion that restorative practices are the panacea to all schools' disciplinary issues (González, 2012). Ensuring schools do not act as institutions that drive the lowest performing students to prison involves more than discipline reform. It requires new decisions around a host of contributing elements: curriculum, pedagogy, and relationship building (Smith, 2015; Wadhwa, 2013).

NECESSARY DISCIPLINE, NECESSARY ACCOUNTABILITY

Broadly, operational rules, standards, and guidelines in schools are necessary. As with any organization, inevitable conflicts of interests, goals, resources, and freedom of action arise. Those individual representatives of the schools' interests, such as teachers and administrators, are obligated to take some action when misconduct disrupts the ongoing function of the organization, in this case, education and instruction. Ideally, discipline as a socialization practice functions not only to curtail disruptive behavior but also to guide and limit organizational members' actions and to instruct and support them in how to care for themselves and others. From the perspective of Wachtel and McCold's (2001) social discipline window, effective discipline combines both accountability and support. In the case of the school setting, often discipline is additionally conceptualized as instructive for (particularly students') lives outside of the school. However, if punishments such as suspensions, detentions, and expulsions are believed to improve the functional environment for school community members, the data seem to suggest otherwise. Out-of-school suspensions or expulsion neither reduce rates of disruption nor improve school climate. Exclusionary discipline practices are simply not effective in reducing problem behavior. Rather, the available data suggest "disciplinary removal appears to have negative effects on student outcomes and the learning climate" (American Psychological Association, 2008 in Minnesota Department of Education, 2012; González, 2012). In short, simply pursuing punishment, which Wachtel and McCold (2001) frame as being high in accountability but low in supportiveness, is deficient.

School expectations of behavior can fall into a number of broad categories including the appropriate use of time, dress, work completion, and social interaction. Because discipline typically involves traditional punishment or consequences for misbehavior, it is often the context in which restorative justice theory makes its way into a school community. However, more recently, a number of conceptualizations of restorative justice in schools are described more broadly with regard to the school "culture" or "climate" (Das, 2017; Howley, 2003; Wadhwa, 2013) Invariably, the central tenets of restorative justice are bound to activate in the wake of misconduct. As we will see, the integration of restorative justice into the school setting has gone beyond proceduralist responses to particular misconduct events. Indeed, the philosophical thrust of restorative practices so contrasts itself with punitive practices, that their integration into multiple levels of the educational context, exemplifying a structuralist approach, should not be surprising. We believe that this marks a paradigmatic shift in considering the role of restoration beyond individual infractions. Indeed, a "whole school" restorative school community would seem to entail certain beliefs about justice, fairness, and the treatment of its community members, which reflect broad values of inclusion, belonging, and the paramount importance of functional, healthy relationships (Davis, 2018). In such a school, restorative practices may even do more before an offence to inculcate a communicative climate of empathy, respect, and support.

Similar philosophical practices have been a system-wide disciplinary goal in Canada for at least ten years. As stated in the Ontario Ministry of Education (2009) document *Making Ontario's Schools Safe: What Parents Need to Know*, safe-schools strategies need to move discipline away from solely punitive responses to an approach that codifies conduct in a manner that corrects inappropriate behavior while offering multiple levels of support for students (both victims and offenders) (Rideout, Karen, Salinitri, & Marc, 2010). Restorative tools presented both a challenge and an opportunity to these Ontario school boards to change their current discipline to support students' growth (Rideout et al., 2010).

O'Callaghan (2005) notes that restorative practices are methods designed to help school community members (staff, students, and parents) to find healthy ways of relating in a variety of contexts, not only limited to discipline, and not only limited to school. One of the challenges facing restorative practices' adoption is the need for a common set of strategies for their implementation. Engaging a restorative discipline program also requires intentionality when cultivating relationships with key stakeholders, such as parents, family members, and other respected support persons (Green et al., 2019). O'Callaghan (2005) further states that in contrast with authoritarian zero tolerance, restorative practices ought to provide high levels of both control *and* support. Students are encouraged to be responsible for their own behavior and to be cocreators of a collaborative conflict response. Restorative practices flourish in schools where authority figures (e.g., teachers and administrators) do discipline *with* students, rather than *to* or *for* them (Rideout et al., 2010).

We have explicated a broad history of Western school discipline and noted the philosophical differences regarding the implementation of restorative justice and, more broadly, restorative practices. For us, restorative practices inform a theory of corrective community building toward a more humane response to hurtful interactions: all individuals are positioned as participants within a community of care, where accountability and personal responsibility are communicatively placed center-stage for the rebalancing of the scales of justice (Rideout et al., 2010). The practices that are further derived have been researched in a seemingly endless parade of case studies. Results are positive, if repetitive.

With a host of both case study and anecdotal evidence pointing to the effectiveness of restorative justice as a discipline-specific practice, school administrators, teachers, researchers, and scholars currently advocate for a school-wide cultural change that aims to prevent misbehavior by focusing on a restorative justice curricula, restorative conversations, circles, and dialogues, and building a restorative ethos (Cameron & Thorsborne, 2001; Hopkins, 2004; International Institute for Restorative Practices, 2010; Monk, 2010; Morrison, 2002; 2005; Morrison, Blood, & Thorsborne, 2005; Riestenberg,

2012). These advocates perceive restorative justice evolving from an isolated tool of disciplinary intervention to a broad spectrum of practices of prevention (Schumacher, 2014). The restorative ethos is a holistic, humanistic, approach grounded in helpful relationships, respectful and attentive communication, and an inclusive, respectful community spirit. Some documents thus employ restorative "practices" or "measures," rather than "justice," to draw a distinction between activities that may be proactive and not simply reactive (as restorative justice almost always is). Restorative justice also connotes to some a criminological, punitively focused juvenile justice program (Karp & Breslin, 2001; McCluskey et al., 2008; Wachtel, 2004). Frequently it seems the terms are used interchangeably in the literature. That so many experts in the field of Western education, both practitioners and researchers alike, see a value for a more restorative set of school-wide practices begs the question of what we now know.

Manifestations of Restorative Discipline/Practices

Communities are made stronger, students made more emotionally intelligent, and relationships grow when schools adopt restorative practices (Amstutz & Mullet, 2005). Before this can happen, however, schools must cease viewing discipline as solely punishment (Paul, 2020). Discipline typically has a number of goals. First, discipline needs to aid in stopping and preventing disruptive behavior. Second, discipline should explain, model, and reinforce what is appropriate. Next, and more long-term, discipline should help to teach self-discipline. Such a major change in the way that schools view discipline is a significant challenge. Punishment continues to dominate the school discipline landscape because it is quick, easily administered, and appears as if at least *something* has been done. Restorative discipline, like punishment, is concerned with providing appropriate consequential responses, which encourage accountability. However, that accountability emphasizes empathy and harm repair (Rideout et al., 2010).

According to Amstutz and Mullett (2005), conflict resolution education, emotional literacy, and character education all came together to form restorative discipline. Together they each affirm that restorative justice promotes values, principles, and behaviors that use inclusive, collaborative approaches for being in a community. The practices foreground authentic communication to resolve disputes between members of a school community. Restorative approaches confirm participant experiences and needs, particularly of those who have been harmed, excluded, or bullied. They facilitate actions and responses that foster healing rather than alienation or coercion. Restorative discipline must be flexible and creative in conflict resolution, character education, and the development of emotional literacy.

The relationship-building component of restorative practices is of paramount importance, it seems, for the operation of these disciplinary systems. As Smith (1998) and Noddings (1995) emphasize, children who connect person-to-person with their teachers are more likely to learn and succeed personally and academically. Amstutz and Mullet (2005) conclude that if a child feels uncared for, they will neither feel safe enough to take academic risks nor will they care enough to resist engaging in disruptive actions. Furthermore, when students see adults treat each other with care, they are more likely both to model the behaviors and to engage actively the restorative practices offered to them (Rideout, Karen, Salinitri, & Marc, 2010).

Under the paradigm of restorative practices, "the operant ideal is relational currencies, not external sanctioning systems" (Morrison & Vaandering, 2012, p. 140). While external sanctions (e.g., those offered by zero tolerance) deprive participants of the opportunity for growth, restorative practices offer students a chance to learn via social connection, inclusion, and viewing pro-social conflict models. There is evidence from a number of states using restorative justice to replace ineffective zero tolerance policies for drug, alcohol, and other offenses (Karp & Breslin, 2008).

In another practice, Ashworth (2008) describes a new-style restorative justice-modeled detention wherein instead of sitting in silence or completing homework, students work with a staff mentor during their detention. The student uses that time to learn to separate unhelpful behavior from his, her, or their own self-worth and to generate options to begin to make amends (Ashworth, 2008). Other restorative practices take on a host of forms: peer juries to reduce suspensions, expulsions, and school referrals to the juvenile courts (Mann, 2016), talking circles as "spaces of healing" (Wadhwa, 2013, p. 97), and anti-bullying programs. Restorative anti-bullying efforts are doubly vital because of both the ineffectiveness of prior disciplinary interventions and the lasting negative impact of being bullied.

Bullying behaviors appear unaffected by school punishment or anti-bullying legislation (Duncan, 2011; Morrison, 2006; Pavelka, 2013; Smith, 2015). Thus, more restorative solutions have included non-violent conflict resolution strategies. These provide a foundation upon which individuals can take positive actions when faced with a bullying situation. These restorative practices help to teach students a spectrum of non-violent conflict communication strategies for use both within and outside the school (Morrison, 2006; Saha, 2012). Furthermore, the benefits of restorative discipline come to all participants: bullies, victims, and bystanders (Pavelka, 2013). Restorative discipline's goals include fostering accountability, creating and exploiting healthy shame, and community-building. Specifically, healthy shame requires encouraging bullies to take responsibility for their actions and to address the harms caused (Morrison, 2006). Herein lies a different process for responding to classic school discipline behavior, one that builds not only a perspective that highlights communication, relationships, and inclusion, but also one that generates novel, beneficial results.

There ought to be caution in the application of restorative practices to bullying discipline. Some researchers are unconvinced. "Whilst it is clear that constructive conflict resolution methods for children teach empathy, increased communication skills, co-operation and respect for each other, whether conflict coaching can be used to decrease bullying in schools remains to be evaluated" (Saha, 2012, p. 126). However, in one evaluation, specifically at the elementary and high school levels, there was statistical evidence of reduced bullying, foul language, racial slurs, fighting, throwing objects, harassment, insubordination, and smoking (Smith, 2015). These results attempt to create a culture of support and more positive relationships. Results of the study are consistent with the underlying philosophy of restorative justice in which restoration and strengthening of relationships is essential for building community in schools (Rideout et al., 2010).

WHAT'S NECESSARY FOR RESTORATIVE PRACTICES

Restorative practices vary by student age (Hopkins, 2011). They have nearly infinite malleability to respond to (and be adapted for) different situations of conflict, especially, but not exclusively, after there's been harm (Amstutz & Mullet, 2005; Morrison, 2007a). Harm communicates that a damaged relationship exists. The participants in restorative practices might interact reactively, such as in victim-offender/bully mediation (Smith, 2015) or in more proactive contexts, such as counseling and adult-student mentorship (Brown, 2015), restorative conferencing, or peacemaking circles (Anfara et al., 2013). The scope can range from whole-school models to system or district-wide implementation, individual classrooms, or an isolated teacher. Almost always a restorative practice lives alongside a punitive system, while most view their philosophies as incompatible (Stinchcomb et al., 2006). Restorative justice is positioned to handle unique cases, circumstances, and myriad opportunities. Restorative disciplinary interactions challenge systemic standardization, consistency, and predictability (Anfara et al., 2013).

A number of researchers and theorists have proposed foundational principles, objectives, and values, which ought to undergird any shift to a restorative set of school practices. According to Khamisa (2005), "The restorative justice model is based on the premise that crime [in this case, student misbehavior] occurs in the context of the community and the community must be involved in addressing it" (p.159). Rundell (2007) asserts, a paradigm shift toward a restorative philosophy requires adherence to five basic principles:

(1) face-to-face participation (2) through cooperation rather than coercion where (3) those affected directly decide the outcome (4) through a just process (5) that is modeled by restorative facilitators' own practices.

Additionally, Anfara et al. (2013) list seven foundational principles as necessary for restorative practices to be considered:

1. *Meet needs.* According to Zehr (2002), these needs include freedom of action, stability, and relatedness. Students attempt to meet these needs through more or less helpful means. Restorative practices seek to give students what they need, not necessarily what they deserve (Vaandering, 2010). Victim needs must be both listened to and responded to (Lockhart & Zammit, 2005).

2. *Provide accountability and support.* In a restorative paradigm, a student who has misbehaved or violated a school rule is called to respond, and a victim is also called to take account of the harm that's been done to him, her, or them. Both offender and victim are thus accountable and connected to the obligations that have been incurred. As opposed to a punitive, adversarial school disciplinary system, restorative practices call victims to a position of strength where accountability is tied to compassion and personal reflection (Lockhart & Zammit, 2005).

3. *Making things right.* Sometimes this is termed "repairing harm," "healing," or "mending" (Howley, 2003). This principle connotes the effects of offending behavior on the self and other community members (Karp & Breslin, 2001). Addressing harms helps offenders and victims discover insights into both sides' feelings and perspectives. Often there is restitution, and the offender develops a plan of response, rather than having the plan thrust upon her, him, or them (Brown, 2015).

4. *Conflict is a learning opportunity.* The opportunity for learning is for emotional and social growth, community building, and the connection with others. Restorative justice models teach pro-social conflict resolution and response techniques (Morrison & Vaandering 2012; Wadhwa, 2013).

5. *Build healthy learning communities.* Restorative practices, done holistically, affect student-student, student-teacher, student-school, as well as teacher-teacher relationships (Suvall, 2009). School communities are built and rebuilt by reintegration and caring support (Lockhart & Zammit, 2005). Rather than a reactive system focused on pupil control, restorative practices focus on dialogue and interaction with the ultimate goal of more functional (school) communities.

6. *Restore relationships.* One of the basic tenets of the restorative paradigm is "since the offender created the problem, then the offender should help solve it" (Khamisa, 2005, p. 162.). Misbehavior can be conceptualized as

a violation of relational expectations as well as a violation of the rules. Presumably, the rules exist to foster healthy relationships and healthy school community environments. Restorative justice clarifies what events have occurred, what effects those events generated, and the resulting needs associated with the effects, and how to redress any resulting harms.

7. *Addressing power imbalances.* Bullying, social inequality, institutional inequality (e.g., as was seen with zero tolerance), suspension and expulsion are a kind of institutionalized violence committed against the student and the community as a whole (Wadhwa, 2013). Restorative practices challenge the system itself (Lockhart & Zammit, 2005). Restorative practices, when they are functioning at their best, call into question the system of discipline itself, how it came to be in place, whose interests it serves, if the school structures are helpful in developing the kinds of young citizens we need or if the school system instead tends to proliferate and perpetuate harm, recrimination, and retribution.

While these objectives may indeed form a cornerstone of restorative research in the school context, there is much work to be done regarding the empirical assessment of their application in actual school systems. Now we turn to a consideration of some of the published research detailing the contexts, methods, and results of restorative practices in an educational context.

Researching the Restorative School

In general, the data on restorative justice programs and restorative practices in schools is poor, with minimal empirical research extant concerning its effectiveness (Green, Willging, Zamarin, Dehaiman, & Ruiloba, 2019). It is fairly well established that more empirical, data-driven research is needed (Morrison & Vaandering, 2012). Most research into restorative justice in schools is institutional, case study, or evaluation reports (Sumner et al., 2010). Perhaps this dearth of empirical data owes its origin to restorative justice theory's application in criminological contexts. Support for restorative discipline is often anecdotal.

Restorative justice theory is inevitably applied in schools differently. Indeed, one of the challenges with restorative justice implementation is the perception of the theory as ill-defined with consensus in its application lacking (Fields, 2003; Morrison & Vaandering, 2012). Results of restorative interventions are almost always positive, such as conclusions, which "reported decreases in major disciplinary issues, reductions in the number of expulsions and out-of-school suspensions, and shifts from expelling students with drug and alcohol issues to providing support that resulted in a reduction in substance abuse" (Anfara et al., 2013, p. 61). Further, school-based models for addiction recovery have been developed, which appear to be both restorative and effective (Marietti, 2015).

In primarily (or exclusively) qualitative research into restorative practices in schools, there is often a connection drawn between restorative justice and critical theory and dialogic insights garnered from philosophers such as hooks and Freire (Barnes, 2015; Vaandering, 2009). The specific goals of these qualitative school studies can be quite different, from developing an after-school program or detention alternative based on restorative justice theory (Ashworth, 2008), to building a proactive program directed at developing students' emotional capacity and emotional needs (Schumacher, 2012).

Research into restorative programs and practices in schools proceeds often by mixing qualitative and quantitative methodologies. An example of the kind of methodological mix that seems typical includes McClusky (2008) who collected two-years of restorative justice evaluation data, compiled from focus groups, interviews with school community members, participant (including student) surveys, policy document analysis, as well as summary data from national school statistical analyses. Wholly quantitative analyses do not seem to be the norm. Case study analysis, typically of only a single school or two, often includes a focus on qualitative data and ethnographic responses.

Strictly quantitative studies are far fewer in number. When quantitative results are presented, they tend to show significant reduction in the number of behavioral infractions, and decreases in school absences (Rideout et al., 2010). Similarly encouraging results were found by González (2012). Over the course of the four-year study, suspensions dropped by 34 percent, school expulsions were reduced by 82 percent and police referrals were down by 72 percent. The author traces these results to the over 800 formal restorative interventions conducted (González, 2012). Program satisfaction is also high (80–85 percent) and greater than 72 percent of participants felt agreements were fully followed (González, 2012). Mann (2016) in a study of restorative peer juries found they promote leadership, accountability, ownership, and civic engagement. After the peer juries were introduced, they were found to increase student attendance and instructional time, decrease discipline problems and negative behavior, and reduce recidivism. Participant feelings of safety, understanding, and acceptance also improved under one restorative paradigm (Suvall, 2009).

While quantitative studies focus on documenting longitudinal changes in misbehavior, and sometimes recidivism, qualitative school studies tend to focus on the more ineffable relationships between participants. Since there is not a measure of positive relationship development between students and school adults, qualitative scholars are left with some difficulty in measuring and documenting the phenomena of most interest to them (González, 2012). Research into restorative practices seems dedicated to a single or several school case study, semi-structured interviews, occasional document analysis, and ethnographic theme development or perhaps a phenomenological analysis (see Arkwright, 2003; Ashworth, 2008; Barnes, 2015; Brown, 2015; Creswell & Poth, 2017; Howley, 2003; Lustick, 2017; Mann, 2016; Marietti, 2015; Richards, 2018). The themes discovered are rarely surprising or critical of the restorative practices under examination. Participants invariably find the process fair, inclusive, beneficial to relationships, often constrained by a presumptive punitive framework, or a punitive expectation from some administrators or teachers. In these types of studies, future research is cut and paste, calling for a larger subject pool and a more diverse sample population (Barnes, 2015; Brown, 2015; González, 2012; Marietti, 2015; Richards, 2018).

Some qualitative studies, though not all, do strive for more empirical validity in their methodology such as Das (2017) in a comparative case study analysis, which drew on a human service organizational theoretical framework, which included face-to-face interviews followed by inductive and deductive software analysis. Curiously, in at least one example (Wadhwa, 2013), there was open researcher resistance to the value of methodological triangulation and empirical reliability so as not to "dilute the analysis" (p. 47).

All told, the research conclusions often note conflict between restorative justice and existing school policies as well as the need for teachers (and others) to demonstrate an observable commitment to restorative policies and its integration into school discipline policy. More traditional punitive school policies seem philosophically at odds with a new restorative justice program. Yet, restorative justice as the core operating theory of a school's discipline policy can help to reinforce more progressive school values, when they align with restorative justice's principles (Cameron & Thorsborne, 1999). The operant mechanism for school change is theorized to be the result of the positively affected relationship-building within the school community (especially for at-risk students) who were perhaps most prone to absence. Additionally, because restorative discipline focuses on the reintegration of the student into the learning community, students are able to feel they have a clean slate once they return to the school (Rideout et al., 2010).

In conclusion, what seems key is for restorative justice to be a visible component of the school ethos. No longer is discipline to be kept a secret, shameful activity done behind the windowless, closed doors of the vice-principal's office. One of the key lessons of restorative justice implementation in schools is the value of justice as at least a semi-public, discussed phenomenon (Wearmouth, McKinney, & Glynn 2007a; 2007b). It seems that when justice (and perhaps an act of restitution) is visible to students and teachers, justice becomes something that helps participants to resolve conflicts before they escalate.

Considerations to Implementation

Given the evidence of the benefits of implementing restorative practices into school contexts, they have experienced significant hurdles to implementation namely time, money, and training. First, systemic changes in school climate requires commitment and time. Three to five years seems typical (Blood & Thorsborne, 2005). It is important to question not only the amount of time a change to restorative practices will take but also the timing of implementation. Hopkins (2002) recommends beginning restorative justice implementation from whichever point the school system finds itself. Often there are teachers or administrators within a district or school who already operate some version of restorative practice. The lesson seems to be to begin where you're at, rather than waiting for an ideal moment of funding, training, or a disciplinary crisis to occur (Anfara et al., 2013). As mentioned previously, one of the key principles of restorative justice is its voluntary nature. Aligning with this philosophical tenet, restorative justice should come into the school with broad teacher buy-in, consultation, training, and agreement (Cameron & Thorsborne, 1999).

Next, funds are needed for training personnel to implement the restorative processes (in whatever form those take) (Suvall, 2009). Restorative justice training needs to be reoriented with fidelity and quality control in mind (Das, 2017). However, in contrasting this claim is Wadhwa (2013) who believes "even without explicit professional development around restorative justice, students and teachers [in circles] implicitly promote the principles of community, egalitarianism, and responsibility" (p. 100).

In terms of effectiveness and efficiency, some questions remain about the investment of time and energy required to make restorative justice work in a school setting, especially if extra-school factors, (e.g., the costs of imprisonment and lack of social mobility for drop-outs) are excised from the disciplinary calculus.

Implications

The punitive model is powerful, long-standing, entrenched and appeals to a certain subset of school community members, parents, and politicians. When schools are deeply steeped in the punitive philosophy of discipline, which also communicates values of centralized authority, hierarchy, and impersonality, their focus toward (and willingness to consider) a practice, which relies less on control, reduced coercive force, and non-violence is significantly diminished. Students can even come to expect the standard, expedited, punitive punishments (Wadhwa, 2013). Standard punishment for standard infractions smacks of a prison sentence. A student may have repeatedly experienced suspension from school, and for that student this is just another ritual. Whereas, something like a healing circle, where pupils sit shoulder-to-shoulder with the classmate they have bullied, can be far more difficult.

In contexts where the punitive culture is strong, initial support for and acceptance of the theory of restorative justice (especially with poorly funded education, implementation, and participant training) is likely to be low. Restorative practices will not thrive in a school, which views students as less-than-worthy of full human consideration and respect. The traditional paradigm emphasizing students' lack of capacity, need for correction, inclination for misconduct, and true desire for strict management and control will always be at odds with restorative justice theory.

Implementation will benefit from strong, powerful leadership combined with broad grassroots support (Anfara et al., 2013). This combination of top-down and bottom-up reform seems to be key in developing the whole school culture and ethos change required for effective implementation (Cameron & Thorsborne, 1999). For restorative programs to work in schools, they require institutional support in terms of resources, space, and training (González, 2012).

Additional research recognizes the critical role community-based organizations play at both the policy and local school adoption levels (Das, 2017). In addition to the role these organizations play, individual school principals hold real power in determining if restorative justice will gain more than a beachhead in any school. "Successful implementation . . . within schools includes three main factors: leadership, effective communication, . . . and invigorating a positive school culture" (Das, 2017, p. xii). Such a culture will only be improved with the adoption of a relational restorative communication perspective, one which makes it clear to students, teachers, and other community members that protecting their identity and sense of belonging is of paramount importance.

As Das (2017) asserts, there should also be some caution levied regarding communication especially as it can result in ineffective program education. Miseducation could cause misunderstanding for those not intimately connected with restorative philosophy, as well as conflict with punitive, school-wide disciplinary mandates. Teachers on the outside of some restorative programs may even view restorative responses as not being enough punishment (Wadhwa, 2013). In this particular case, because restorative circles were not practiced throughout the building, there grew animosity between teachers' efforts to respond to conflicts restoratively and the broader school-wide approach which favored punitive measures.

Pedagogically, Morrison (2007) suggests that restorative justice implementation happen across three levels. First, whole-school efforts focusing on developing and re-affirming a community of respect and openness.

This is precisely the type of proactive use of restorative justice theory and restorative practices we have thus far considered. Second, relational repair at the level of peer-group conferencing, teacher circles, small-group mediations. Finally, the third level is that which focuses on isolated harm-generating events. These result in a traditional victim-offender conference.

What kinds of discipline do we want in school? "Answering the question should involve rigorous conversations about the purpose of education, and what kind of competencies we want our students to take away from their schooling" (Wadhwa, 2013, p. 164). The evidence seems to show restorative disciplinary practices support student learning, emotional growth, and conflict management skills, without heavy-handed punishment (Smith, 2015). Restorative practices are naturally at odds with the American cultural values of speed, standardization, and predictable conformity "for all intents and purposes restorative justice developed as a community based movement established in direct opposition to the large-scale, institutional way of doing business" (Erbe, 2004, p. 293). It seems broader cultural resistance to restorative programs can be expected.

Some of the cultural and racial dynamics endemic to the American school complicate implementing restorative practices. Discipline (even restorative discipline) is typically used as a tool of control and reactive response. In this manner, it may have the tendency to reproduce some of the traditional inequalities apparent in punitive discipline, especially when administrators skirt the role racism, sexism, and other prejudices play. For restorative practices to work against this kind of discrimination, three factors seem necessary: (a) a staff committed to discussing broader social issues and their impact on students; (b) professional development around culture, discipline systemic racism and implicit bias; and (c) funding that supports the first two (Lustick, 2017). Finally, if restorative justice practices are not positioned to "address the structural and institutional influences acting on school participants, . . . [it will be] reduced to a decontextualizing, skill-building exercise for managing conflict at the level of the behaviour of students in schools'' (Vaandering, 2009, p. iii).

For researchers, the literature analysis here conducted seems to show clearly there is very little need for additional theoretical understanding. Continual reiterative projects within a narrow case study aimed at defining restorative philosophy or principles, at discovering themes, or uncovering insights is to walk retrod, well-cleared ground. Examining the philosophy and psychology of power underlying punitive systems may be interesting to gain more buy-in from new restorative justice practitioners/participants.

Some key stakeholders within the school system could be further tapped for their insights and harnessed for their value in restorative practices. For instance, school counselors' experiences, need for training, and function as trainers may be necessary in the school to maintain restorative practices

(Richards, 2018). Perhaps this will lead to greater professionalization of restorative practitioners (Wadhwa, 2013). Lastly, practice should consider and integrate the current conceptual buzzword of sustainability, which seems key in terms of developing something like a critical mass for trained practitioners, onboard politicians, and policymakers (Vaandering, 2009).

REFERENCES

Advancement Project. (2010). Test, punish, and push out: How "zero tolerance" and high-stakes testing funnel youth into the school-to-prison pipeline. https://b.3cdn. net/advancement/50071a439cfacbbc8e_suxm6caqe.pdf.

Alexander, M. (2012). *The new Jim Crow: Mass incarceration in the age of colorblindness* (Rev ed.). New Press.

American Psychological Association Zero Tolerance Task Force. (2008). Are zero tolerance policies effective in the schools? An evidentiary review and recommendations. *American Psychologist, 63*(9), 852–862. https://doi.org/10.1037 /0003-066X.63.9X852.

Amstutz, L. S. (2015). *The little book of restorative discipline for schools: Teaching responsibility; creating caring climates*. Simon and Schuster.

Amstutz, L.S., & Mullet, J. (2005). *The little book on restorative discipline for schools*. Good Books.

Anfara Jr, V. A., Evans, K. R., & Lester, J. N. (2013). Restorative justice in education: What we know so far. *Middle School Journal, 44*(5), 57–63. https://doi.org/10.1 080/00940771.2013.11461873.

Arkwright, F. N. (2003). Restorative justice in the Solomon Islands. In S. Dinnen, A. Jowitt & T. Newton Cain (Eds.), *A Kind of Mending: Restorative Justice in the Pacific Islands* (pp. 177–194). Pandanus Books.

Ashworth, J. A. (2008). *A case study of comprehensive schoolwide improvement at a high needs elementary school*. [Unpublished doctoral dissertation. University of South Dakota.

Barnes, D. S. (2015). *Restorative peacemaking circles and other conflict management efforts in three Ontario high schools*. [Unpublished doctoral dissertation]. University of Toronto.

Blood, P., & Thorsborne, M. (2005, March). The challenge of culture change: Embedding restorative practice in schools. Paper presented at the Sixth International Conference on Conferencing, Circles and other Restorative practices, Sydney, Australia.

Bowlby, J. (1969). Attachment and loss v. 3 (Vol. 1). Random House. Furman, W., & Buhrmester, D. (2009). Methods and measures: The network of relationships inventory: Behavioral systems version. *International Journal of Behavioral Development, 33*, 470–478. https://doi.org/10.1.

Brendtro, L., & Larson, S. (2004). The resilience code: Finding greatness in youth. *Reclaiming children and youth, 12*(4), 194–200. https://mosesmadison.org/wp-co ntent/uploads/2016/03/The-Resilience-Code_-Finding-Greatness-in-Youth.pdf.

Brown, M. A. (2015). *Talking in circles: a mixed methods study of school-wide restorative practices in two urban middle schools.* [Unpublished doctoral dissertation]. Florida Atlantic University.

Cameron, L., & Thorsborne, M. (1999, February). Restorative justice and school discipline: Mutually exclusive? Paper presented at the Reshaping Australian Institutions Conference. Australian National University, Canberra, Australia.

Cameron, L., & Thorsborne, M. (2001). Restorative justice and school discipline: Mutually exclusive? In H. Strang & J. Braithwaite (Eds.), *Restorative justice and civil society* (pp. 180–195). Cambridge University Press.

Cavanagh, T. (2009). Book review: Working restoratively in schools., 2012, from http:// www.restorativejustice.com/Book%20Reviews.html.

Creswell, J. W., & Poth, C. N. (2017). *Qualitative inquiry and research design: Choosing among five approaches.* Sage Publications.

Das, A. (2017). *From the margins to the mainstream? A comparative case study of restorative justice implementation and integration within public schools.* [Unpublished doctoral dissertation]. The University of Chicago.

Davis, F. E. (2018). Whole school restorative justice as a racial justice and liberatory practice: Oakland's journey. *The International Journal of Restorative Justice, 1*(3), 428–432. https://doi.org/10.5553/IJRJ/258908912018001003007.

Dignity in Schools. (2009). Fact sheet: School discipline and the push out problem. https://dignityinschools.org/resources/dsc-created-fact-sheets/.

Drakeford, W. (2006). Racial disproportionality in school disciplinary practices. National Center for Culturally Responsive Educational Systems. http://www.nccrest.org/Briefs/School_Discipline_Brief.pdf.

Duncan, S. (2011). Restorative justice and bullying: A missing solution in the antibullying laws. *New England Journal on Criminal & Civil Confinement, 37*(2), 267–298. https://heinonline.org/HOL/P?h=hein.journals/nejccc37&i=271.

Erbe, C. (2004). What is the role of professionals in restorative justice? In H. Zehr, & B. Toews (Eds.), *Critical issues in restorative justice* (pp. 293–302). Criminal Justice Press.

Fabelo, T., Thompson, M. D., Plotkin, M., Carmichael, D., Marchbanks III, M. P., & Booth, E. A. (2011). *Breaking schools' rules: A statewide study of how school discipline relates to students' success and juvenile justice involvement.* Report prepared by the Council of State Governments Justice Center.

Fields, B. A. (2003). Restitution and restorative justice in juvenile justice and school discipline. *Youth Studies Australia, 22*(4), 44–51. https://search.informit.com.au/documentSummary;dn=818178860885200;res=IELHSS.

González, T. (2012). Keeping kids in schools: Restorative justice, punitive discipline, and the school to prison pipeline. *Journal of Law & Education, 41*(1), 281–336. https://heinonline.org/HOL/P?h=hein.journals/jle41&i=285.

Green, A. E., Willging, C. E., Zamarin, K., Dehaiman, L. M., & Ruiloba, P. (2019). Cultivating healing by implementing restorative practices for youth: Protocol for a cluster randomized trial. *International journal of educational research, 93*, 168–176. https://doi.org/10.1016/j.ijer.2018.11.005.

Hopkins, B. (2002). Restorative justice in schools. *Support for Learning, 17*(3), 144–149. https://doi.org/10.1111/1467-9604.00254.

Hopkins, B. (2004). *Just schools: A whole school approach to restorative justice.* Jessica Kingsley Publishers.

Hopkins, B. (2011). *The restorative classroom: Using restorative approaches to foster effective learning.* Optimus Education.

Howley, B. P. (2003). Restorative justice in Bougainville. In S. Dinnen with A. Jowitt & T. Newton (Eds.), *A kind of mending: Restorative justice in the Pacific Islands* (pp. 215–254). ANU E Press.

Human Rights Watch. (April 2009). US: Prison numbers hit new high. http://www.hrw.org/en/reports/2008705 704/targeting-blacks.

International Institute of Restorative Practices (2010). Restorative practices: Whole School implementation. The 11 essential elements. http://www.iirp.edu/pdf/SSS_Implementation_Overview.pdf.

Karp, D. R., & Breslin, B. (2001). Restorative justice in school communities. *Youth & Society, 33*(2), 249–272. https://doi.org/10.1177/0044118X01033002006.

Khamisa, A. (2005). *From murder to forgiveness* (2nd ed.). ANK Publishing, Inc.

Latimer, J., Dowden, C., & Muise, D. (2005). The effectiveness of restorative justice practices: A meta-analysis. *The Prison Journal, 85*(2), 127–144. https://doi.org/10.1177/0032885505276969.

Lockhart, A., & Zammit, L. (2005). *Restorative justice: Transforming society.* Couto Printing.

Lustick, H. (2017). "Restorative justice" or restoring order? Restorative school discipline practices in urban public schools. *Urban Education,* 1–28. https://doi.org/10.1177/0042085917741725.

Mann, J. M. (2016). *Peer jury: School discipline administrators' perceptions of a restorative alternative to suspension and expulsion.* [Unpublished doctoral dissertation]. Hampton University.

Marietti, P. M. (2015). Breaking the Cycle of Drug Abuse: A Case Study of Latino Students in a Recovery Classroom in Relation to Healing and Restorative Justice Practices. [Unpublished doctoral dissertation]. California Lutheran University.

McCluskey, G., Lloyd, G., Stead, J., Kane, J., Riddell, S., & Weedon, E. (2008a). "I was dead restorative today": From restorative justice to restorative approaches in school. *Cambridge Journal of Education, 38*(2), 199–216 https://doi.org/10.1080/03057640802063262.

McCluskey, G., Lloyd, G., Kane, J., Riddell, S., Stead, J., & Weedon, E. (2008b). Can restorative practices in schools make a difference? *Educational Review, 60*(4), 405–417. https://doi.org/10.1080/00131910802393456.

McKown, C., & Weinstein, R. S. (2002). Modeling the role of child ethnicity and gender in children's differential response to teacher expectations. *Journal of Applied Social Psychology, 32*(1), 159–184. Retrieved from: https://doi.org/10.1111/j.1559-1816.2002.tb01425.x/abstract.

Minnesota Department of Education (2012). Alternatives-to-Suspension Grant: Progress Report—Year 2. http://education.state.mn.us/mdeprod/idcplg?IdcSer

vice=GET_FILE&dDocName=040309&RevisionSelectionMethod=latestRelea
sed&Rendition=primaryTheOhioSenate(2013).

Monk, G. (2010, October). Building a restorative practice curriculum in middle and high schools in the U.S. Paper presented at the 13th World Conference of International Institute of Restorative Practices, Hull, England. http://www.iirp.edu/ pdf/Hull-2010/Hull-2010-Monk.pdf.

Morrison, B. (2002, February). Bullying and victimization in schools: A restorative justice approach (Report # 219). http://www.aic.gov.au/ 272.

Morrison, B. (2005). Restorative justice in schools. In E. Elliott & R. Gordon (Eds.), *New directions in restorative justice* (pp. 26–52). Willan.

Morrison, B. (2006). School bullying and restorative justice: Toward a theoretical understanding of the role of respect, pride, and shame. *Journal of Social Issues, 62*(2), 371–392. https://doi.org/10.1111/j.1540-4560.2006.00455.x.

Morrison, B. (2007). *Restoring safe school communities: A whole school response to bullying, violence and alienation.* Federation Press.

Morrison, B., Blood, P., & Thorsborne, M. (2005). Practicing restorative justice in school communities: The challenge of culture change. *Public Organization Review: A Global Journal, 5,* 335–357 https://doi.org/10.1.

Morrison, B. E., & Vaandering, D. (2012). Restorative justice: Pedagogy, praxis, and discipline. *Journal of School Violence, 11*(2), 138–155 https://doi.org/10.1080/1 5388220.2011.653322.

O'Callaghan, E. (2005, March). The Mackillop model of restorative practice. Paper presented at Building a Global Alliance for Restorative Practices and Family Empowerment, Part 3. IIRP's Sixth International Conference on Conferencing Circles and other Restorative Practices, Penrith, NSW, Australia.

Paul, G. D. (2020). Cultivating a space for restorative justice in Kansas: Exploring opportunities for restorative justice through dialogic deliberation. In P. M. Kellett, S. L. Connaughton, & G. Cheney (Eds.), *Transforming conflict and building peace: Community engagement strategies for communication scholarship and practice* (pp. 133–160). Peter Lang.

Pavelka, S. (2013). Practices and policies for implementing restorative justice within schools. *Prevention Researcher, 20*(1), 15–17.

Richards, E. A. (2018). An Exploration of School Counselors' Experience with Restorative Practices. [Unpublished master's thesis]. California State University, Long Beach.

Rideout, G., Karen, R., Salinitri, G., & Marc, F. (2010). Measuring the impact of restorative justice practices: Outcomes and contexts. *Journal of Educational Administration and Foundations, 21*(2), 35–60.

Riestenberg, N. (2012). *Circle in the square: Building community and repairing harm in school.* Living Justice Press.

Rudd, T. (2014). Racial disproportionality in school discipline: Implicit bias is heavily implicated. Kirwan Institute for the Study of Race and Ethnicity. http://kirwaninstitute. osu. edu/wp-content/uploads/2014/02/racial-disproportionalityschools-0 2. pdf.

Rundell, F. (2007). "Re-story-ing" Our Restorative Practices. *Reclaiming Children and Youth, 16*(2), 52. https://cyc-net.org/cyc-online/cyconline-july2010-rundell.ht ml.

Saha, P. (2012). Conflict coaching: A tool for conflict resolution in schools. *James Cook University Law Review, 19*, 113–126. https://heinonline.org/HOL/P?h=hein .journals/jamcook19&i=113.

Schumacher, M. A. (2014). Talking circles for adolescent girls in an urban high school: A restorative practices program for building friendships and developing emotional literacy skills. *Sage Open, 4*(4). https://doi.org/10.1177/21582440145 54204.

Skiba, R. J., Michael, R. S., Nardo, A. C., & Peterson, R. L. (2002). The color of discipline: Sources of racial and gender disproportionality in school punishment. *The Urban Review, 34*(4), 317–342. https://doi.org/10.1023/A:1021320817372.

Smith, A. (2015). *Bullying resilience: Informing schools and communities to transform conflict by using an anti-bullying restorative justice campaign.* [Unpublished doctoral dissertation]. Capella University.

Stinchcomb, J. B., Bazemore, G., & Riestenberg, N. (2006). Beyond zero tolerance: Restoring justice in secondary schools. *Youth Violence and Juvenile Justice, 4*(2), 123–147. https://doi.org/10.1177/1541204006286287.

Sumner, M. D., Silverman, C. J., & Frampton, M. L. (2010). School-based restorative justice as an alternative to zero tolerance policies: Lessons from West Oakland. Thelton E. Henderson Center for Social Justice. Berkeley, CA: University of California, Berkeley, School of Law.

Suvall, C. (2009). Restorative justice in schools: Learning from Jena High School. *Harvard Civil Rights-Civil Liberties Law Review, 44*, 547–569. https://heinonline .org/HOL/P?h=hein.journals/hcrcl44&i=551.

U.S. Department of Justice, Civil Rights Division and the U.S. Department of Education, Office of Civil Rights (2014). Dear colleague letter: Nondisciminartory Administration of School Discipline. http://www.justice.gov/crt/about/edu/docume nts/dcl.pdf.

Vaandering, D. D. (2009). *Towards effective implementation and sustainability of restorative justice in Ontario public schools: A critical case study.* [Unpublished doctoral dissertation]. University of Western Ontario.

Vaandering, D. (2010). The significance of critical theory for restorative justice in education. *The Review of Education, Pedagogy, and Cultural Studies, 32*(2), 145–176. https://doi.org/10.1080/10714411003799165.

Wadhwa, A. (2013). *Race, discipline, and critical restorative justice in two urban high schools.* [Unpublished doctoral dissertation]. Harvard University.

Wald, J., & Losen, D. (May 16–17, 2003). Defining and redirecting a school-to-prison pipeline: Framing paper for the school-to-prison pipeline Research conference. Northeastern University's Institute on Race and Justice.

Wearmouth, J., McKinney, R., & Glynn, T. (2007b). Restorative justice in schools: A New Zealand example. *Educational Research, 49*(1), 37–49. https://doi.org/10 .1080/00131880701200740.

Zehr, H. (2002). Journey to belonging. In E. G. M. Weitekamp & H. Kerner (Eds.), *Restorative justice: Theoretical foundations* (pp. 21–31). Will.

Chapter 5

Constituting Community through Restorative Justice

As discussed in the preceding chapters, the concept of community plays a central role in restorative justice research, discourse, and practice (Newbury, 2008; Pavlich, 2002; Rossner & Bruce, 2016; Walgrave, 2002; Zehr, 2002). In the restorative justice literature, community has been identified as a stakeholder that experiences harm (Rossner & Bruce, 2016), a group of people close to victims or offenders (e.g., "communities of care," Bolivar, 2010), and a set of relationships (McCold & Wachtel, 1998). It also has been framed in the literature as a principle, ideal, or rhetorical concept that ought to guide and inform the practice and conceptualization of restorative justice (Rossner & Bruce, 2016; Walgrave, 2002).

The fluidity of community coincides with the reframing of the role/place of community in the context of restorative justice. Lewis and Umbeit (2020) argue that "issues of race, social conditions, historical harm, and community systems are taking center stage in the restorative world" (p. 4). In making this argument, they identify several "shifts" in the focus of restorative justice and restorative practices. These shifts roughly correspond to conventional, proceduralist and constitutive, structuralist framings of restorative justice. In discussing the place of restorative justice in communities, modern conceptualizations of restorative justice have begun to widen (if not outright move) the focus from programs to community organizing, focusing on "incorporat[ing] restorative practices into everyday life" (Wachtel & McCold, 2001, p. 115). In this chapter, we use Procter's (2006) framework of community and work on deliberative democracy to situate both structuralist and proceduralist approaches to restorative justice as inherently democratic concepts that intersect with peacemaking and community transformation. We explore this focus and its implications for structural change and restorative practice.

FRAMEWORKS OF COMMUNITY

Procter (2006) identifies three conceptualizations of community: (1) community as territory, (2) community as relational, and (3) community as symbolic. Community as territory is a place-based conceptualization of community, framing community in terms of a defined area or location, such as a neighborhood. When restorative justice practitioners describe their work "in communities," they typically are using this territorial framing. A relational framing of community highlights the psychological connection or unity among community members. It is this sense that underlies Block's (2008) notion of community as "sense of belonging." Relational community provides a feeling of connection and interdependence with others, akin to microcommunities (McCold, 2004). Community as symbolic calls attention to the linguistic, communicative construction of community. Rather than separating out language from community, this perspective frames community as a product of language, interaction, and meaning. This perspective coincides with a constitutive perspective of communication by foregrounding interpretive processes inherent in words, performances, behaviors, and other rhetorical artifacts that help to (re)construct the governing ideologies of communities.

The framework identified by Procter (2006) corresponds with the multiple ways community has been framed in the restorative justice literature: as stakeholders, locations, and relationships. As a stakeholder, community may play the role of victim harmed by an offense, a neutral third party there to help offenders take responsibility for their actions, or members who can be involved in restorative processes (Rossner & Bruce, 2016). For example, Johnstone (2002) writes that "community must be prepared to be involved in the resolution of conflicts between offenders and victims, in supporting victims and in supporting and monitoring offenders" (p. 14). Braithwaite (1999) likewise identifies "community participation and community caring" (p. 6) as central restorative justice values. In terms of location, community has been defined as an area in which restorative justice programs operate. This "community-of-place" conceptualization (Willis, 2016) aligns with Procter's definition of community as territory in which we think about community in terms of its geographic boundaries or areas of service. "Community" also has been framed relationally, whether as "communities of care" and "micro-communities" or as the sense of belonging that develops through dialogue. This relational framing, what Willis (2016) calls "community-of-care," highlights the relationship strengthening consequences of restorative practices, such as through shows of social support, rituals of reintegration, and practices of convening. A symbolic perspective of community, in turn, asks us to turn our attention to ways in which restorative justice and community emerge through language and symbols. The remainder of this chapter explores this switch, in line with Lewis and Umbreit's (2020) discussion of restorative justice shifts. As a continuation of our exploration of the contexts in which restorative justice is emerging (families, schools, and online), we discuss the restorative justice-community relationship both programmatically and communally, focusing on how the adoption of restorative justice values and programs works to constitute community.

COMMUNITY THROUGH RESTORATIVE JUSTICE

In their discussion of the growth of restorative justice within communities, Green, Johnstone, and Lambert (2013) begin in the 1970s and trace the growth of victim-offender mediation (VOM) and proliferation of other types of restorative justice programs (e.g., family group conferencing, neighborhood accountability boards) that fall under the larger umbrella of restorative justice. These programs tended to emerge within a particular context (the criminal justice system) to address specific types of harm (criminal wrongdoing by youth). Over time, the types of harm and contexts addressed through restorative justice expanded. Restorative justice programs began to be used in schools, families, and workplaces to address historical harm and trauma. As Green et al. (2013) note, this expansion coincided with a shift in the language of restorative justice toward an emphasis on "practices," "processes," and "approaches."

Underlying this expansion, Green et al. (2013) contend, is a common theme of communication. At the core of relarional harm is "communication breakdown" and its effects on "understanding, tolerance, empathy, and belonging" (Green et al., 2013, p. 454). One approach they identify is addressing communication breakdowns through dialogic processes such as VOM, peace circles, and conferences. Such a programmatic or proceduralist recommendation aligns with a relational perspective of community that aims to restore relationships and a sense of belonging through dialogic communication as well as a territorial perspective of community that highlights the growth of restorative justice programs within particular communities. Consequently, the growth of programs focused on restorative justice as "peacebuilding", "conflict resolution," and the like (as discussed earlier) is partly a function of organizations aiming to address communication breakdowns within their communities. This approach takes somewhat of a conventional perspective of communication, together with territorial and relational perspectives of community to the work of peacemaking. By developing skills in empathic and dialogic communication within a particular setting (e.g., school, family, organization), the idea is to build stronger relationships among people, thereby developing a more closely knit community.

From a systemic perspective, a constitutive perspective of communication can be helpful for both understanding and constructing community. In essence, the central tenet of this perspective is that the ways in which we communicate—our patterns, discourses, texts, interpretations, and meanings—constitute our idea and experience of community, which means that the evolution of restorative justice and community are at their cores functions of communication. For example, Block (2008) describes community using a discourse of restorative justice that emphasizes dialogue, connectedness, possibility, and empowerment. By tracing the constitution of community through communication, we create an opening for the development of discourses and practices that are rooted in values associated with restorative justice.

While this can be evident in many corners of community life, we focus here on the implications of democratic decision-making practices on membership and organizing. As Dzur and Wertheimer (2002) note, "Theories of restorative justice and deliberative democracy both place public communicative action at center stage" (p. 6). We highlight deliberative democracy not only because of the communicative practices associated with democratic decision-making but also because of its constitutive consequences related to membership and belonging.

Community Governance and Decision-Making

Democratic approaches to governance often are contrasted with "bureaucratic," "managerialist," or "representative" approaches to decision-making in which a small group of people make decisions for the whole without the engagement or involvement of most community members (Spano, 2001). Political scientists might accurately describe such a system as an oligarchy. This small group may be elected officials, boards of directors, executive committees, or similar small groups. Moreover, when citizens do get involved, they tend to speak within their enclaves (like-minded people), rather than with those with whom they do not see eye to eye, perpetuating a divide that manifests itself in fractured identity politics; competitive, win-lose decision-making; and dehumanizing others. Even in the cases of engaging with dissimilar others, asynchronous communication practices through social media channels can create more of a talking *at* rather than a talking *with* feel.

Deliberative democracy, however, is about public, collective decision-making in which all or the majority of stakeholders take responsibility for the choices that directly affect them (Gastil, 2014; Kim & Kim, 2008; Parkinson & Roche, 2004). This type of governance focuses on bringing citizen stakeholders together to generate decisions that need to be made, often through facilitated deliberation, dialogue, and discussion. Deliberative democracy encourages citizens "to feel safe to take risks and speak genuinely, [meaning that] people need to have the opportunity to participate in shared life" (Longo & Shaffer, 2019, p. 15). Spano (2001) distinguishes between strong/participatory democracy and thin/representative democracy in terms of involvement and inclusivity. Representative democracy, which is more closely tied with our conventional bureaucratic systems, is characterized by a reliance on those in positions of power to generate solutions and then have citizens vote on the acceptance or rejection of those solutions. Participatory democracy, however, fosters active cooperation, involvement, and inclusivity through practices such as deliberation and dialogue. Such an approach aligns with dialogic practices to attend both to relational needs and to shared decision-making needs through deliberative processes. Eisenberg, Trethewey, LeGreco, and Goodall (2017) describe dialogue as communication that is mindful, equitable, empathic, and respectful of others. Deliberation, in turn, involves collective decision-making on public issues (Black, 2008; Longo & Shaffer, 2019). Such decision-making can take place using a variety of facilitated techniques that help people to weigh evidence and share perspectives on issues. This combination of dialogue, deliberation, and ongoing conversation ideally enhances all people's voice, promotes listening, builds trust, and incorporates diverse perspectives to make effective decisions and promote community cohesion (McCoy & Scully, 2002).

These emphases on accountability, voice, listening, trust, and facilitated collective decision-making parallel elements of restorative justice (Kidder, 2007; Parkinson & Roche, 2004; Ritchie & O'Connell, 2001; Stout & Salm, 2011). For example, Block (2008) describes a restorative community as being a function of "citizens' willingness to own up to their contribution, to be humble, to choose accountability, and to have faith in their own capacity to make authentic promises to create the alternative future" (p. 48). Likewise, restorative processes such as victim-offender conferences, family group conferences, and truth and reconciliation commissions have been described as promoting accountability among all stakeholders (Braithwaite, 2002; Morris, 2002; Umbreit & Ritter, 2006; Wachtel & McCold, 2001), facilitating meaningful participation in the justice process (Daly, 2016; Dzur & Wertheimer, 2002; Sivasubramaniam & Goodman-Delahunty, 2006), enabling dialogic communication that involves the sharing of perspectives (Armour & Umbreit, 2006; Braithwaite, 1999; Paul, 2017), and repairing trust (Lewis & Umbreit, 2015; Paul & Dunlop, 2014).

In sum, restorative justice and deliberative democracy share similar ideological principles emanating from the communicative root concept of *voice*. They emphasize collective decision-making in which all stakeholders are meaningfully involved in sharing and considering one another's experiences to make decisions together. This co-creative, dialogic communication ideally results in (re)building trust that facilitates continued sharing and collaboration among stakeholders.

Membership and Belonging

Connected to the idea of collectivity in deliberative democracy is the issue of membership. Whereas bureaucratic governance limits those who are allowed into conversations, deliberative democracy strives to be more inclusive through its aim to create space for all interested stakeholders to share their voice in the decision-making process. This inclusiveness is a key feature of restorative justice as well, both in terms of formal processes and in terms of systems involvement. Yet, as Paul (2016) notes, this aim for inclusive membership paradoxically can produce a strong in-group / out-group force that marginalizes those who do not share similar value systems as those being advocated.

Both Zehr (2002) and Block (2008) highlight the importance of a sense of belonging for individuals within a community. Zehr (2002) describes belonging through the metaphor of journeying, arguing that "alienation as well as its opposite—belonging—are central issues for both those who offend and those who are offended against" (p. 21). Victimization and its ensuing trauma problematize people's interpretations of their own identities, the harm-doer's identities, and the nature of the world around them. Offending, likewise, symbolically undermines values that were supposedly shared among people within the larger community (Wenzel & Okimoto, 2010). This undermining can communicate that the offender does not share those same values, throwing into question the offender's standing (belonging) in that community. Thus, an important focus of restorative practices is the reaffirmation of community values through positive accountability practices such as apologies, involvement of those who can reaffirm community values, forgiveness, and reconciliation (Armour & Umbreit, 2016; Braithwaite, 2016; Newbury, 2008; Paul & Borton, 2017; Wenzel, Okimoto, Feather, & Platow, 2010). Such apologies and involvement help to foster a renewed sense of empowerment and belonging for all parties while simultaneously emphasizing the importance of maintaining community belongingness (Paul, 2016).

While Zehr (2002) frames the questions of belongingness largely around the perspective of the victim, Block's (2008) approach to belongingness flows from the larger questions of community membership and how communities should function structurally. Block argues that "community exists for the sake of belonging and takes its identity from the gifts, generosity, and accountability of its citizens" (p. 30). A citizen, in turn, "is one who is willing to be accountable for and committed to the well-being of the whole" (p. 63). This connection between the whole and the constitutive parts is reminiscent of Wachtel and McCold's (2001) social discipline window that describes restorative discipline as being high in both control and support. Control and support presuppose mutual accountability—accountability of the individual to the whole (control) and the whole to the individual (support). For Block, community and the sense of belonging are functions of collective, ongoing conversation that enables continued transformation.

In essence, the issue of membership and belonging, from a restorative perspective, is one of inclusion and integration. Inclusivity and meaningful involvement are rooted in practices such as apologies given by offenders, reintegrative acts performed by victims, transformative conversations among community members, and processes that welcome all voices. These communicative practices, in the form of storytelling and dialogue, facilitate the co-construction of shared identities as they explore one another's experiences (Black, 2008). After all, identity is a communicative construct, emerging over time through conversation and interpretation (Scott, 2007).

One additional note is worth mentioning on this subject of belonging, however. While deliberative democracy and restorative justice share a common emphasis on inclusion, this is not to say that there is not exclusion in restorative justice. Both Pavlich (2005) and Paul (2016) discuss this "paradox of community" that occurs when the push toward inclusivity also results in the exclusion of those who appear to reject the ideology of the whole. For example, refusing to apologize and accept responsibility for wrongdoing, being unwilling to offer restitution, or continuing to violate communal expectations for behavior can communicate that a person does not share the same fundamental attitudes, values, beliefs, and opinions as the whole. When this happens, collectives with a strong commitment to belonging may resort to exclusion as a way to protect themselves and their ideologies. In workplaces, this can look like firing employees who are not "team players." In communities, this can look like shunning, ostracizing, or imprisoning those who do not abide by or embrace communal norms. In small groups, groupthink and self-censorship can occur, which can be seen as the product of not wanting to signal divergence from the group and risk violating the unity of the group. Such in-group / out-group tendencies can emerge when there is an emphasis on the maintenance of a strong collective identity—an emphasis that emerges as community belongingness becomes more important. In short, inclusion and exclusion are meaningful and constitutive of one another.

IMPLICATIONS FOR CONSTITUTING RESTORATIVE COMMUNITIES: A CASE STUDY OF ORGANIZING

The parallels of deliberative democracy and restorative justice prompt us to ask the question: How do we create systems that foster collective decision-making and belongingness? This shift to a systems-level perspective of organizing is a hallmark of a structuralist perspective of restorative justice that draws attention not only to specific programs but rather to the integration and interdependence of individual parts, relational patterns, and governing principles. It is this perspective, for example, that Davis (2018) takes when discussing the process of "restorganising" within the Oakland (CA) school system, writing:

> We have been intentional about implementing a parallel strategy of providing restorative services at school sites while simultaneously "restorganising" to achieve systems change affecting all schools. This has entailed both a bottom-up and top-down organizing approach, meaning we do on-the-ground work with students, their families, educators and others while also engaging in advocacy for systems change with policy makers. (p. 429)

These themes of involvement, advocacy, and systems change were evident in a series of conversations in Kansas about ways to incorporate restorative justice into community systems (Paul, 2020). Drawing on Davis' and Paul's reported experiences, we identify a number of implications for the work of constituting community through restorative justice.

Study the System

Part of implementing a system guided by restorative justice values is getting to know the systems that make up a community. Paul (2016), drawing on the bona fide group's perspective, argues that one of the limitations of conventional restorative justice research is its failure to account for contexts in which restorative justice processes and organizations are operating. This context includes the different systems—political, legal, economic, sociocultural, and more –that give meaning to community life.

Studying systems means identifying stakeholders who make up those systems, understanding the relationships among those stakeholders, and getting a feel for how systems operate over time. For example, Paul (2020) discusses how the community effort in Kansas relied on the identification of key stakeholders who were involved in areas such as the school system, the justice system, and other community organizations to get the process started. Following this initial step of identifying stakeholders, an additional helpful step is to map the system to explore how groups are connected with one another. A key principle of systems is *holism*, or the idea that the whole is greater than the sum of its parts. Identifying relationships that are positive, relationships that are contrient, or even the lack of an existing relationship where one could/ should be can be helpful in understanding how and why communities are operating the way they are.

Involve Stakeholders throughout the Community

In describing the work in Oakland, Davis (2018) writes, "The essence of restorative justice involves shifting the locus of power from systems and professionals to community and ordinary people" (p. 430). While this statement suggests a problematic dualism that seems to underlie some restorative justice work (Paul & Borton, 2017), inherent in it is a key point about the importance of involving stakeholders throughout the community rather than focusing solely on policy makers or people in positions of conventional authority.

Such involvement should be widespread and diverse, with the aim of including as many perspectives as possible. For example, involved in the Kansas conversations were nonprofit directors, educators, youth, law enforcement officers, judges, and other interested community members. Involving diverse groups of citizens facilitates the sharing and consideration of multiple perspectives and experiences that can enhance decision-making, planning, and storytelling.

Develop Opportunities for Collective Dialogic Deliberation

Connected with the step of involving many stakeholders is the step of designing effective processes that enhance voice, facilitate perspective-taking, and empower people to develop support systems rooted in restorative justice values. Such processes are rooted in dialogic deliberation—a facilitated decision-making process that enables people to develop and share multiple perspectives, experiences, and types of information while making concrete decisions on opportunities and questions. This sharing creates what Black (2008) calls "dialogic moments"—"fleeting, typically unplanned, instances where partners experience being both present and open to the other's experience" (p. 98). It is in this step of designing dialogic deliberative processes that there is a turn from an adversarial orientation fed by dualistic thinking toward a democratic orientation guided by dialectical thinking.

Develop Systems That Will Foster Continued Involvement

One potential pitfall in designing restorative systems is the failure to plan for what's next. There is a tendency in change efforts to focus on short-term implementation—framing issues, convening groups, facilitating conversations, and developing an action-plan that identifies next steps. Yet, systems are oriented toward inertia, meaning that systems are likely to resist short-term efforts toward change.

Systemic change requires persistent efforts aimed not only at fostering particular actions but also at developing new language and attitude sets. Promoting one without the other will be superficial and short-lived: programs with symbolic shifts will die off without a clear understanding for their need, symbolic shifts without behavior change will leave observers wondering "so what." Both Senge (1990) and Block (2008) address the need for change in interpretive lenses in their discussion of systems and communities. For Senge, this discussion revolves around "mental models," or ways of understanding the world around us. For Block, this discussion revolves around "context," which provides meaning for our experiences. Both concepts draw attention to the role of interpretation and language—that is, community as symbolic. Working to sustain long-term shifts in both behavior and interpretive lenses that are rooted in restorative ideologies at the individual, relational, organizational, and societal levels can create and reinforce mutually sustaining restorative systems that generate restorative community.

REFERENCES

Armour, M. P., & Umbreit, M. S. (2006). Victim forgiveness in restorative justice dialogue. *Victim and Offenders, 1*(2), 123–140. https://doing.org/10.10.1080/1 5564880600626080.

Black, L. W. (2008). Deliberation, storytelling, and dialogic moments. *Communication Theory, 18*(1), 93–116. https://doing.org/10.1111/j.1468-2885.2007.00315.x.

Block, P. (2008). *Community: The structure of belonging.* Berrett-Koehler Publishers.

Bolívar, D. (2010). Conceptualizing victims' "restoration" in restorative justice. *International Review of Victimology, 17*(3), 237–265. https://doi.org/10.1177/0 26975801001700301.

Braithwaite, J. (1999). Restorative justice: Assessing optimistic and pessimistic accounts. In M. Tonry (Ed.), *Crime and justice: A review of research* (vol. 25, pp. 1–127). University of Chicago Press. https://doi.org/449287.

Braithwaite, J. (2002). Setting standards for restorative justice. *British Journal of Criminology, 42*(3), 563–577. https://doi.org/10. 1093/bjc/42.3.563.

Daly, K. (2016). What is restorative justice? Fresh answers to a vexed question. *Victims & Offenders, 11*(1), 9–29. https://doi.org/10.1080/15564886.2015.11 07797.

Davis, F. E. (2018). Whole school restorative justice as a racial justice and liberatory practice: Oakland's journey. *The International Journal of Restorative Justice, 1*(3), 428–432. https://doi.org/10.5553/IJRJ/258908912018001003007.

Dzur, A. W., & Wertheimer, A. (2002). Forgiveness and public deliberation: The practice of restorative justice. *Criminal Justice Ethics, 21*(1), 3–20. https://doi.org /10.1080/0831129X.2002.9992112.

Eisenberg, E. M., Trethewey, A., LeGreco, M., & Goodall, H. L. Jr. (2017). *Organizational communication: Balancing creativity and constraint* (8th ed.). Bedford/St. Martin's.

Green, S., Johnstone, G., & Lambert, C. (2013). What harm, whose justice?: Excavating the restorative movement. *Contemporary Justice Review, 16*(4), 445–460. https://doi.org/10.1080/10282580.2013.857071.

Johnstone, G. (2002). *Restorative justice: Ideas, values, debates.* Willan.

Kim, J., & Kim, E. J. (2008). Theorizing dialogic deliberation: Everyday political talk as communicative action and dialogue. *Communication Theory, 18*(1), 51–70. https://doi.org/10.1111/j.1468-2885.2007.00313.x.

Lewis, T., & Umbreit, M. (2015). A humanistic approach to mediation and dialogue: An evolving transformative practice. *Conflict Resolution Quarterly, 33*(1), 3–17. https://doi.org/10.1002/crq.21130.

Lewis, T., & Umbreit, M. (forthcoming). Are we serving victims well? Considerations on victim engagement in restorative justice movement trends. https://zehr-institute.org/publications/docs/chapter-10.pdf.

Longo, N. V. & Shaffer, T. J. (2019). Discussing democracy. In N. V. Longo & T. J. Shaffer (Eds.), *Creating space for democracy: A primer on dialogue and deliberation in higher education.* Stylus.

McCold, P., & Wachtel, B. (1998). Community is not a place: A new look at community justice initiatives. *Contemporary Justice Review, 1*(1), 71–85. https://doi.org/.

McCold, P. (2004). Paradigm muddle: The threat to restorative justice posed by its merger with community justice. *Contemporary Justice Review, 7*(1), 13–35. https://doi.org/10.1080/1028258042000211987.

McCoy, M. L., & Scully, P. L. (2002). Deliberative dialogue to expand civic engagement: What kind of talk does democracy need? *National Civic Review, 91*(2), 117–135. http://ncdd.org/rc/wp-content/uploads/2010/08/McCoy-DD_Expand_CE.pdf.

Morris, A. (2002). Critiquing the critics: A brief response to critics of restorative justice. *British Journal of Criminology, 42*(3), 596-615. https://doi.org/10.1093/bjc/42.3.596.

Newbury, A. (2008). Youth crime: Whose responsibility? *Journal of Law and Society, 35*(1), 131–149. https://doi.org/10.1111/j.1467-6478.2008.00418.x.

Parkinson, J., & Roche, D. (2004). Restorative justice: Deliberative democracy in action? *Australian Journal of Political Science, 39*(3), 505–518. https://doi.org/10.1080/10361404200295101.

Paul, G. D. (2016). A bona fide group perspective of restorative justice: Implications for researchers and practitioners. In P. M. Kellett & T. G. Matyok (Eds.), *Transforming conflict through communication in personal, family, and workplace relationships* (pp. 125–130). Lexington Books.

Paul, G. D. (2017). Paradoxes of restorative justice in the workplace. *Management Communication Quarterly, 31*(3), 380–408. https://doi.org/10.1177/0893318916681512.

Paul, G. D. (2020). Cultivating a space for restorative justice in Kansas: Exploring opportunities for restorative justice through dialogic deliberation. In P. M. Kellett, S. L. Connaughton, & G. Cheney (Eds.), *Transforming conflict and building peace: Community engagement strategies for communication scholarship and practice* (pp. 133–160). Peter Lang.

Paul, G. D., & Borton, I. M. (2017). Toward a communication perspective of restorative justice: Implications for research, facilitation, and assessment. *Negotiation and Conflict Management Research, 10*(3), 199–219. https://doi.org/10.1111/ncmr.12097.

Paul, G. D., & Dunlop, J. (2014). The other voice in the room: Restorative justice facilitators' constructions of justice. *Conflict Resolution Quarterly, 31*(3), 257–283. https://doi.org/10.1002/crq.21091.

Pavlich, G. (2002). Deconstructing restoration: The promise of restorative justice. In E. G. M. Weitekamp and H-J Kerner (Eds.), *Restorative justice: Theoretical foundations* (pp. 90–109). Portland, OR: Willan.

Pavlich, G. (2005). *Governing paradoxes of restorative justice.* Glasshouse Press.

Procter, D. E. (2006). *Civic communion: The rhetoric of community building.* Rowman & Littlefield.

Rossner, M., & Bruce, J. (2016). Community participation in restorative justice: Rituals, reintegration, and quasi-professionalization. *Victims & Offenders, 11*(1), 107–125. https://doi.org/10.1080/15564886.2015.1125980.

Scott, C. R. (2007). Communication and social identity theory: Existing and potential connections in organizational identification research. *Communication Studies, 58*(2), 123–138. https://doi.org/10.1080/10510970701341063.

Senge, P. M. (1990). *The fifth discipline: The art and practice of the learning organization.* Doubleday/Currency.

Sivasubramaniam, D., & Goodman-Delahunty, J. (2006). Trust and power-distance: A psychological perspective on fairness in restorative justice conferences. *Psychiatry, Psychology and Law, 13*(2), 203–219. https://doi.org/10.1375/pplt.13.2.203.

Umbreit, M. S., & Ritter, R. (2006). Arab offenders meet Jewish victim: Restorative family dialogue in Israel. *Conflict Resolution Quarterly, 24*(1), 99–109. https://doi.org/10.1002/crq.160.

Wachtel, T., & McCold, P. (2001). Restorative justice in everyday life. In H. Strang & J. Braithwaite (eds.), *Restorative justice and civil society* (pp. 114–129). Cambridge University Press.

Walgrave, L. (2002). From community to dominion: In search of social values for restorative justice. In E. G. M. Weitekamp and H-J Kerner (Eds.), *Restorative justice: Theoretical foundations* (pp. 71–89). Willan.

Wenzel, M., & Okimoto, T. G. (2010). How acts of forgiveness restore a sense of justice: Addressing status / power and value concerns raised by transgressions. *European Journal of Social Psychology, 40*(3), 401–417. https://doi.org/10.1002/ejsp.629.

Wenzel, M., Okimoto, T. G., Feather, N. T., & Platow, M. J. (2008). Retributive and restorative justice. *Law and Human Behavior, 32*, 375–389. https://doi.org/10.1007/s10979-007-9116-6.

Zehr, H. (2002). Journey to belonging. In E. G. M. Weitekamp and H-J Kerner (Eds.), *Restorative justice: Theoretical foundations* (pp. 21–31). Willan.

Chapter 6

Restorative Justice in Digital Spaces

Our longstanding relationships almost always include conflict at some point and on some level; this is even more so of those relationships most important to us. Intimate relationships, those marked by closeness in a workplace, school, or family are almost guaranteed to, in some measure, involve the perception of incompatible goals, scare resources, interference from others, and differing needs (Wilmot & Hocker, 2007). The traditional models of restorative practices almost exclusively presume an in-person, face-to-face (FtF) meeting between conflict stakeholders. Some even claim it is a requirement (Rundell, 2007). Even in cases where FtF interaction is not explicitly required, it is frequently conceptualized as the ideal restorative setting.

This expectation, however, stands in stark contrast with the needs of restorative justice programs to provide a low-cost, safe, efficient, effective, and transformative mediation experience for their participants. The opportunities for victims and offenders, workplace collaborators, and even disparate family members to meet virtually in computer-mediated communicative (CMC) restorative encounters has grown in this first part of the twenty-first century. The value of FtF interaction between victim and offender (perhaps the most fundamental hallmark of a restorative process) is challenged by the ever-growing public expectation that interpersonal interactions can be accomplished just as well via our smartphones. This expectation became a need for many communities and restorative service providers beginning in the spring of 2020 when the global pandemic of COVID-19 brought social distancing, the shuttering of non-essential businesses, and the closure of many schools and universities.

Since communication constitutes the mode by which we come to understand ourselves, others, and the world around us, we feel it is vital to consider how adopting a restorative perspective grounded in communication can inform novel ways of implementing restorative justice theory into the digital world. In this chapter, we review the theoretical debate around the capacity of "virtual" encounters to satisfy the goals of restorative justice, profile a number of programs' digital services, and provide best-practice recommendations based on interviews representing a cross-section of American restorative justice programs.

There is a long history of scholarship over the past forty years attesting to the inappropriateness of CMC to address the complex needs of an interpersonal conflict. This, so-called, "cues-filtered-out approach" (Culnan & Markus, 1987; Rice & Case, 1983; Steinfield, 1985; Williams, 1977) argues that communication channels, which include more (and more synchronized) nonverbal cues, allow us to communicate the warm, complex messages we expect to experience from human interactions. According to this theoretical lens, mediated communication will be less effective than "richer" FtF communication for handling conflicts because it cannot provide a needed level of breadth and depth of nonverbal cues on which people rely when managing conflict.

By contrast, other CMC perspectives, such as the social information processing (SIP) theory (Walther & Burgoon, 1992), claim that the relative dearth of nonverbal cues in CMC means it can be used to construct more beneficial, intimate sets of relationships as people adjust their expectations to the constraints and capabilities of new communication technologies. Asynchrony, for example, can allow a couple managing a conflict via text messages to more fully consider, edit, and review their responses before hitting "send," an option unavailable in FtF conversations. The "chat" function in some popular video conferencing software allows participants to ask questions of a speaker in real time without audible interruption, another capacity challenging to mimic in FtF conferencing. In a fairly limited study of several dozen undergraduate students roleplaying a boss/employee scenario, Shin et al. (2017) found no significant difference in the physiological arousal of participants in the FtF versus CMC scenarios. Participants in the FtF scenario reported significantly higher levels of emotional arousal. Further, video chat participants (i.e., CMC) reported their partners as more trustworthy and likable, reported greater conversation satisfaction, and proved more able to judge their partner's emotional arousal than in the face-to-face condition (Shin et al., 2017).

In our view, what is of most concern is not whether or not restoration and dialogue can occur via CMC. Rather, we focus on the consequences—individual, relational, and symbolic—of restorative processes that take place exclusively via CMC. There are multiple scenarios in which even the initial offence may occur online, such as cyber-bullying. If a victim, offender, and community meet virtually through some networked CMC application, there are a number of questions such a scenario begs: Will the offender feel, admit, and express culpability and responsibility for his, her, or their actions? Can such a dialogue result in a victim feeling supported, heard, and compensated for the damage that was done? Can the community representatives express sanction, support, and structure onto a mediated encounter of victim and offender who may live thousands of miles apart and have never interacted in-person? The digital world challenges the understanding of what restorative processes should look like, how they should function, and what we can expect their outcomes to be as they inevitably move into more virtual spaces. Indeed, restorative practicioners are sometimes already faced with choosing a digital space in which to attempt the goals of reconciliation and restoration or choosing no space at all.

Understandably, restorative processes, so many of them rooted philosophically (if not historically) in our shared human past, may be challenged by the common expectations and experiences of our digital present. We wish to carefully consider how new media technologies and ancient restorative practices interact currently and what this may say for the future of restorative justice and technology. We continue with a historical consideration of the "community," and how new technologies have impacted our conceptualization of it.

COMMUNITY AND COMPUTER-MEDIATED COMMUNICATION

There have been a host of academic research studies dedicated to analysis of the community aspect of restorative justice (Maglione, 2017). As described previously, the images held of "community" are socially constructed and play an important role in our understanding of what makes for a complete and valid restorative process. More vitally, as "community" is frequently included in the formulation of restorative justice policies and laws, it is important to consider how the our current, twenty-first century understanding of the communities of which we are a part may be different from how they were initially conceptualized when the restorative justice policies were written and enacted. Previous considerations of the community component of restorative justice seem to provide either normative definitions or elucidation of how community works within the context of a restorative process. As was critiqued in our analysis of restorative justice literature in education, innumerable qualitative case studies are of little help with their tendency toward deep description rather than empirical testing or theoretical model building.

Connected with Procter's (2002) conceptualization framework of community, there seems to be five relevant factors regarding the role of community to consider. "(1) community as stakeholder; (2) community involvement and participation; (3) restoring communities; (4) reintegrating into the community" and (5) the community as the location where justice is done (Maglione, 2017, p. 456). First, the community is frequently regarded as a co-equal member in a restorative process (along with victim and offender). Community members have a stake in the process and outcome of a violation, crime, or an incident, which requires restoration for things to be "made right." The relationship between the community's role in a restorative process and the community's role in more traditional systems of jurisprudence is that of participant to observer. The community "is incorporated into mainstream criminal justice practice only in abstract, highly formalized ways" (Dzur & Olson, 2004, p. 93). In this way, the community, as conceptualized in restorative justice, is partial owner of the offending behavior. This is hypothesized to remove the state from its ownership of the crime and return the responsibility for the crime's response to the community itself (Umbreit, 1994). Can we imagine a scenario where an individual's online community takes the responsibility for responding to misbehavior restoratively?

Second, community involvement frequently takes the form of either direct participation by those affected (e.g., neighbors and family members) or as indirect representatives or proxies for directly impacted individuals (e.g., conflict mediators, sentencing circle participants, and community reparation board members). The goals here are increased participation and widened perspectives in the context of the offense (Maglione, 2017). Frequently, the role of the community in restorative practices is represented by mediators from local community dispute resolution agencies

Third, the community may be another victim and therefore be in need of restoration, itself. When crime or misbehavior is performed in such a way as brings insecurity, fear, or threats upon not only a single individual, but a whole community, then the community, itself, can be thought of as a victim (Maglione, 2017). A series of data breaches, for instance, might directly impact thousands of credit card holders, but cause seemingly an entire industry or economic sector to feel under threat. In such a circumstance, the community may be in need of very different processes and services than in a conflict, which takes place solely IRL. The unprecedented social changes surrounding COVID-19, which began in late 2019/early 2020, left many community members feeling victimized, traumatized, isolated, and in need of restoration.

Fourth, after community needs have been addressed, offenders are theorized to benefit most from restorative justice when she, he, or they are reintegrated into the community. In restorative justice's view, since the misbehavior began within the network of social relationships, it is that network (and their expected support) that will best hold offenders to account for their behavior, support victims as they process the offense's aftermath, and work to reintegrate both into full community membership (Marshall, 1999). What might this mean for typical online behavior, such as blocking, muting, and banning participants from some online forum? How are violators of community norms to be shamed and reintegrated into such a fluid, malleable, and porous a community?

Fifth and finally, the community is almost always written about as if it were a local participant. The community is thought of as surrounding the victim and offender. It is theorized to imbue them with a community standard of conduct. "The local community is aware of needs, interests, beliefs and dangers which threaten the social order and is therefore able to offer remedies or support in the determination and application of solutions responsive to the direct stakeholders' situation" (Shin, Jang, & Bente, 2017, p. 459). Do these classic descriptors fail to capture the nature of an online community, whose members may be spread across the globe, never interact in-person, and may provide very little in terms of psychological support or victim awareness?

It seems invaluable to consider how the fundamental qualities of restorative communities are served and challenged by the current media landscape. Video chat software (such as Skype, Gotomeeting, and Zoom) boast hundreds of millions of registered users (Shin et al., 2017). Such technologies are currently being employed nationally and internationally to mediate disputes, check in on participants, craft solutions and agreements, and continue the work of restoring peace to communities. Additionally, more users on such platforms means at least more opportunities for conflict. Video chat users in long-distance relationships, for instance, report a high frequency of conflicts when communicating over these services (Neustaedter & Greenberg, 2011). This has not stopped a variety of restorative service providers from inventing novel ways to employ such services to deliver peace to their stakeholders.

Distressingly, a number of research findings support the notion that CMC and FtF conversation result in different conflict management styles. The theoretical explanation is that CMC's lack of nonverbal cues (or their asynchrony) is responsible for this difference. Drolet and Morris (2000) compared phone and FtF conversations and found FtF better at rapport development and that FtF participants were more quickly able to settle their conflict. When groups using text chats are studied, they are observed using a more competitive, forcing conflict style than those in a FtF interactions (Zornoza, Ripoll, & Peiro, 2002). Some of the criticism is technical. Video chats limit participants to a single view of their conversation partner(s), typically a portrait-style view of the head and shoulders, leaving many nonverbal cues absent. Turn-taking cues, eye contact, and intimacy development can all be hindered when conversations are conducted via CMC video chats (DePaulo et al., 2003; Shin et al., 2017).

Results are not so completely one-sided, however. Several studies (see Heath & Luff, 1991; Hobman, Bordia, Irmer, & Chang, 2002) report that after initial differences in communicator style, participants tend to adjust their communicative practices in CMC to account for the level of nonverbal cues. This, in turn, allows them to more gracefully facilitate their CMC conversations. Also, "findings suggest that when conversation topics are very personal or potentially problematic for their image or relationship, people feel more comfortable with a channel that provides a distance from the other party" (Shin et al., 2017, p. 3). Would such a distance facilitate or frustrate reintegrative shaming and restoration with a community? It seems when conversations are potentially face threatening, there may be a tendency for people to prefer CMC to FtF. Perhaps it is emotionally less taxing. This would seem to hold implications for behaviors in a restorative process designed to bring together intimately connected victims, offenders, and community members. One restorative justice circle program representing the U.S. Ninth District Court put it this way:

> Technology layers on another obstacle . . . consider a conventional wedding versus a virtual ceremony with bride and groom in different states, or getting together for a game night versus on-line gaming. Even mediation, as typically taught and practiced, largely disregards unity and reduces interactions to an "interest-based negotiation" between parties, largely working to "settle disputes" rather than resolving conflict and strengthening relationships. In this mindset, face-to-face gatherings are perhaps less critical.

A key issue for practitioners to consider is their priorities when conducting their services online. It may be appropriate for some mediation services such as initial participant screening, interviewing, and intake and less so for creating spaces of openness and honesty, respect, caring, accountability, and unity.

Inherent in a restorative encounter is face threat and the expectation of face negotiation for all members of that meeting. Offender(s) are typically asked to recall the events of the offense as well as their mental state at the time. If restorative processes are to be engaged, offenders are called to account for the negative impact(s) their behaviors have caused, and to consider what they might do to make the situation as right as possible. All of these are potentially threatening to the offender's sense of positive and negative face. On the victim's side, they are often also asked to recount the events, potentially touching upon strong negative emotions such as shame, fear, and anger. Victims might further be asked to consider and to ask the offender for reparations or restitution, a clear threat to the offender's autonomy/negative face. Finally, the community is charged with the reintegration of both victim and offender into full participation and membership. Each of these processes and responsibilities strikes us as face negotiation, in which both victim and offender belonging/positive face needs to be constructed, communicated about, and supported as fully as is appropriate.

Some restorative settings occur between victims of crimes of severe violence and thus the FtF meeting between victim and offender may involve a very deeply held fear of physical threat, making them all the more delicate context for conversation (Shin et al., 2017). Herein lies a potential benefit of increased use of CMC in restorative settings. They're safer. There's little chance of physical violence between victim and offender if each participates from the comfort and convenience of their home. If participants have the technological resources and capabilities, it also removes any danger in participant travel, potential infection, or lack of facility accessibility. One restorative justice service provider from the U.S. Tenth District Court told us all home visits and participant check-ins have begun to be conducted via video conference. Before COVID-19, the organization had been sending (a minimum of) two volunteer mediators into participants' homes to conduct pre-conference screenings, potentially opening them up to a variety of unsafe conditions. Those screenings are now conducted wholly virtually.

Individual experiences and technological realities challenge the requirement that restorative encounters be FtF. In fact, there are some advantages to CMC, which confront the theoretical underpinnings of the cues-filtered-out approach. They suggest, for one, that more nonverbal cues are not always advantageous. Indeed, strictly FtF encounters can be worse than a similar CMC encounter for certain relational outcomes and overall communicative satisfaction (Shin et al., 2017). With video chat being used for certain legal proceedings already, their role in restorative practices will only increase. It seems a CMC meeting can provide participants with a safer, less emotionally arousing channel for interaction. The question remains whether that will be an overall net gain or loss to the desired outcomes of FtF restorative processes. On the one hand, the physical and emotional distance provided in a CMC context may facilitate some level of additional participation while simultaneously failing to engender the kinds of deep emotional connection that often accompanies restorative work. Working completely remotely, one restorative program worker in Colorado lamented to us the loss of emotional expression she often saw during and especially after restorative justice processes, when people were congregating together.

The use of video conferencing technology for restorative justice services provides a number of functions unavailable in FtF encounters. Virtual waiting rooms or "lobbies" allow mediators to sequester participants apart from one another until the meeting is ready to begin. All participants can be admitted simultaneously, alleviating any risk that one party or another would feel "territorial" over the mediation space. The lack of physical travel has meant that participation has been easier for many. Perhaps, though, too easy. One limitation of videoconferencing identified by a program in the U.S. Second District Court is the inability to know for certain who is (and who is not) in the room, leading to potential breaches of confidentiality. Further, because of the lack of nonverbal immediacy and physical proximity to participants, there may be an increased risk for potentially dangerous unexpected escalations. In general, it seems that in times where FtF meetings are impossible, or less than optimal, programs have moved to simpler, less severe cases, cases in progress, or cases where items of mutual interest can be agreed upon by shuttle diplomacy.

DIGITAL RESTORATIVE EDUCATION

As a response to global social distancing measures, restorative service providers from Arizona to Colorado to Kansas have been called to provide online-only webinars and trainings to school districts and local communities in conflict resolution practices. However, even this restorative justice education is not without its potential problems. In their analysis of the various modalities of teaching restorative justice (online, hybrid, and FtF), Gilbert, Schiff, and Cunliffe (2013) insist that restorative values and principles must undergird any attempts to teach about restorative justice. For them, restorative justice values culminate in a primary classroom principle to create "a psychological climate based on mutual respect, collaborative learning, mutual trust, supportiveness, openness, authenticity, joy in learning, self-discovery, acceptance and humanness" (Gilbert, Schiff, & Cunliffe, 2013, p. 56). This principle may be a challenge for instructors of online or hybrid (a combination of online and in-person) restorative justice courses. Research seems to show students who join an online course under the impression that it will be easier or less work might adopt positions of minimal participation in the course dialogues and interactions, for instance. In such circumstances, Gilbert and colleagues (2013) advocate behaviors amounting to reintegrative shaming (Braithwaite & Roche, 2001). Through this, the instructor can restate expectations about participation, individual students' accountability to classmates, and consequences on their colleagues of their lack of participation. A restorative conversation between teacher and learner about community expectations for future participation could allow minimally participatory students to learn both *about* restorative justice and also experience the power of reintegration into the broader learning community.

Consider a scenario wherein students in a fully online course have an interaction via one of the course's message boards in which one student employs ill-chosen, offensive language. The instructor is contacted via email by several students in the course uncomfortable with their classmate's language choices. They ask the instructor to do something.

How ought the instructor to proceed? Is the instructor capable in such a scenario of bringing stakeholders together, of communicating community disapproval to the offending student, of restoring the learning community, and of extracting an effective apology? Effective apologies (1) acknowledge the harm that was done; (2) offer an explanation for the offender's behavior; (3) express shame, remorse, or regret; and (4) present options for reparation (Lazare, 2005).

Our contention is that in such a scenario, the instructor ought to honor the highest principles of restorative justice in as holistic, mindful, and humanistic a manner possible. First, even if the instructor has done no work in establishing a restorative discipline scheme for his, her or their classroom, there remain a number of elements, which facilitate communicative interactions between classroom community members. Email, message board communications, and phone-calls are all likely possible in such a scenario. The instructor should first make contact with the student who made the ill-chosen comments and have a conversation wherein they ask about what the student was thinking when writing the comments, who could have been affected by their choices, and what they feel could be done to repair the harm. Next, the instructor should indicate their intention to hold a class conference call or video chat with any interested students (stakeholders) and ask for the offending student's participation. Third, the instructor should schedule and facilitate a class-wide CMC conversation modeled on sentencing circle best practices and expectations. These expectations would ideally be developed and shared with the class before such an incident.

Even in the wake of wrongdoing, the instructor has the ability to communicate clear expectations that in such a discussion respect, listening, empathy, courageous expression, non-judgment, kindness, and open-mindedness will be practiced by all participants. By this process, the intention is to communicate to the class the restorative values of acceptance, authenticity, mutual respect, openness, supportiveness, self-discovery, and humanness (Gilbert, Schiff, & Cunliffe, 2013).

Community restorative justice groups, such as one in the U.S. Eighth District, also saw their services called into action during quarantine to respond to police reports of a surge in domestic violence. They were tasked with creating and facilitating all-digital anger management classes as one response to the influx. One program in the Eastern end of the Tenth District Court provides biweekly community conversations about self-care, trauma, and conflict, weekly anger management courses for "recently returned citizens" on probation or parole, and weekly support meetings for teachers in their local school districts. All told, the unprecedented and immediate need for programs and practices to quickly move to an all-digital format has been accompanied by significant growing pains for communities of restorative practitioners. Taken from a program in the U.S. Ninth District Court, several best practices have emerged to approximate restorative FtF interactions:

1. Enable video whenever possible,
2. Find safe, quiet spaces for participation,
3. Strive to ensure confidentiality in the choice of space (and ideally the use of headphones or earbuds),
4. Disable "chat" features to encourage focus on the speaker,
5. Follow (to the greatest degree possible) your standard structure, format, guidelines, and good speaking/listening expectations for participants.

MOVING AHEAD WITH DIGITAL RESTORATIVE JUSTICE

Restorative practices are grounded in the idea that joining together victim, offender, and community in a very particular process will reap positive outcomes for all. At this point, the theoretical lenses that consider how restoration functions have yet to fully consider how digitization will impact key outcomes. However, in the post-pandemic reality, many organizations around America found that adhering to their core values, and the core values of restorative practices (e.g., listening, participation, healing, and accountability) allowed them to creatively navigate the waters of turbulent times. The cues-filtered-out approach indicates that the partially asynchronous, comparably cold, and mechanical CMC will limit participants' abilities to emotionally engage and benefit from restorative encounters. By contrast, it has been suggested that it is precisely the emotional distance, which will allow some individuals to engage in a restorative process more fully. It is yet to be seen what sorts of outcomes organizations will experience from this shift to digital delivery.

It would be far too premature to assert that restorative justice via CMC is equivalent to FtF restorative encounters. It is not, however, a context to be ignored. In all likelihood, restorative processes will continue to thrive in more digital spaces, potentially exposing many more individuals to the power and challenge of restorative work in their lives. Already many programs in the United States have found novel methods of continuing to engage their stakeholders in a period of prolonged social isolation distancing.

Finally, as virtual reality systems enter into more homes, places of work, and schools, it seems increasingly likely that they will at some point be used for the mediation of conflicts, opening new possibilities for the connection and integration of offenders back into communities of care, and giving victims safer modalities for contact with those who have offended against them. It is an avenue ripe for thorough research and empirical investigation. We believe studies into the function of restorative justice via CMC will reward restorative justice theory greatly in terms of its ability (1) to identify and quantify the mechanisms by which restorative justice works, (2) to clarify the nature and role of community, and (3) to teach online educators how to integrate restorative discipline into their online and hybrid courses.

REFERENCES

Braithwaite, J., & Roche, D. (2001). Restorative justice and responsibility. In M. Schiff & G. Bazemore (Eds.), *Restorative community justice*. Anderson.

Culnan, M. J., & Markus, M. L. (1987). Information technologies. In F. M. Jablin, L. L. Putnam, K. H. Roberts, & L. W. Porter (Eds.), *Handbook of organizational communication: An interdisciplinary perspective* (pp. 420–443). Thousand Oaks, CA: Sage.

DePaulo, B. M., Lindsay, J. J., Malone, B. E., Muhlenbruck, L., Charlton, K., & Cooper, H. (2003). Cues to deception. *Psychological Bulletin, 129*(1), 74–118. https://doi.org/10.1037/0033-2909.129.1.74.

Drolet, A. L., & Morris, M. W. (2000). Rapport in conflict resolution: Accounting for how face-to-face contact fosters mutual cooperation in mixed-motive conflicts. *Journal of Experimental Social Psychology, 36*(1), 26–50. https://doi.org/10.1006/jesp.1999.1395.

Dzur, A. W., & Olson, S. M. (2004). The value of community participation in restorative justice. *Journal of Social Philosophy, 35*(1), 91–107. https://doi.org/10.1467-9833.2004.00218.x.

Gilbert, M. J., Schiff, M., & Cunliffe, R. H. (2013). Teaching restorative justice: Developing a restorative andragogy for face-to-face, online and hybrid course modalities. *Contemporary Justice Review, 16*(1), 43–69. https://doi.org/10.1080/10282580.2013.769305.

Heath, C., & Luff, P. (1991). Disembodied conduct: Communication through video in a multi-media office environment. In J. A. Konstan, E. H. Chi, & K. Hook (Eds.), *Proceedings of the SIGCHI conference on human factors in computing systems* (pp. 99–103). https://doi.org/10.1145/108844.108859.

Hershock, P. D. (2019). Against individualism, for relationalism: Toward an ideal of human becoming committed to relational justice. *Philosophy East and West, 69*(1), 29–39. https://muse.jhu.edu/article/724192.

Hobman, E. V., Bordia, P., Irmer, B., & Chang, A. (2002). The expression of conflict in computer-mediated and face-to-face groups. *Small Group Research, 33*(4), 439–465. https://doi.org/10.1177/104649640203300403.

Lazare, A. (2005). *On apology*. Oxford University Press.

Maglione, G. (2017). Communities at large: An archaeological analysis of the "community" within restorative justice policy and laws. *Critical Criminology, 25*(3), 453–469. https://doi.org/10.1007/s10612-017-9349-8.

Pali, B. (2014). Art for social change: exploring restorative justice through the new media documentary "Inside the Distance." *Restorative Justice, 2*(1), 85–94. https://doi.org/10.5235/20504721.2.1.85.

Marshall, T. F. (1999). *Restorative justice: An overview*. London: Home Office, Research Development and Statistics Directorate.

Neustaedter, C., & Greenberg, S. (2011). Intimacy in long-distance relationships over video chat. In J. A. Konstan, E. H. Chi, & K. Hook (Eds.), *Proceedings of the SIGCHI conference on human factors in computing systems* (pp. 753–762). ACM Press. https://doi.org/10.1145/2207676.2207785.

New Zealand: University offering free online course on restorative justice. (2018). *MENA Report,* Retrieved //aquinas.idm.oclc.org/login?url=https://search-proquest-com.aquinas.idm.oclc.org/ docview/2027377592?accountid=8340.

Rice, R. E., & Case, D. (1983). Electronic message systems in the university: A description of use and utility. *Journal of Communication, 33*(1), 131–152. https://.doi.org/10.1111/j.1460-2466.1983.tb02380.x.

Shin, S. Y., Jang, J. W., & Bente, G. (2017). The benefits of distance and mediation: How people react to conflicts in video chat vs. FtF. *Computers in Human Behavior, 73*, 1–8. https://doi.org/10.1016/j.chb.2017.03.022.

Steinfield, C. W. (1985). Dimensions of electronic mail use in an organizational setting. *Academy of Management Proceedings, 1985*, 239–243. https://doi.org/10.5465/AMBPP.1985.4979313.

Umbreit, M. (1994). *Victim meets offender: The impact of restorative justice and mediation.* Willow Tree Press.

Walther, J. B., & Burgoon, J. K. (1992). Relational communication in computer mediated interaction. *Human Communication Research, 19*(1), 50–88. https://doi.org/10.1111/j.1468-2958.1992.tb00295.x.

Williams, E. (1977). Experimental comparisons of face-to-face and mediated communication: A review. *Psychological Bulletin, 84*(5), 963–976. https://doi.org/10.1037/0033-2909.84.5.963.

Wilmot, W. & Hocker, J. (2007). *Interpersonal conflict* (9th ed.). McGraw-Hill Higher Education.

Zornoza, A., Ripoll, P., & Peiro, J. M. (2002). Conflict management in groups that work in two different communication contexts: Face-to-face and computer mediated communication. *Small Group Research, 33*(5), 481–508. https://doi.org/10.1177/104649602237167.

Chapter 7

Asking Questions of
Restorative Justice

Considerations for Future Growth

The past several decades have witnessed invigorating growth in the practice of restorative justice in various settings. As restorative justice programming has evolved, so too have conceptualizations about the wider systemic implications of a structuralist approach to restorative justice. This growth not only has led to new opportunities but also has spurred on a surge in research on restorative justice (e.g., see evaluative reviews by Hansen and Umbreit, 2018; and Umbreit, Coates, and Vos, 2004), as well as a number of meta-analyses (e.g., Bradshaw, Roseborough, & Umbreit, 2006; Latimer, Dowden, & Muise, 2001; Mullane, Burrell, Allen, & Timmerman, 2014). While the specific questions have varied, there have been at least two general themes among those questions.

One theme is largely conceptual and descriptive, focusing on the nature, dimensions, and inner workings of restorative justice. Such research tends to ask questions such as: what is restorative justice, what are the deontic/ideological principles of restorative justice, what outcomes does restorative justice lead to, what counts as a restorative justice process, how does restorative justice work, how does restorative justice compare with "conventional" or "retributive" justice, and what happens in restorative justice processes (Bazemore & Walgrave, 1999; Braithwaite, 1999; Daly, 2016; Doolin, 2007; Marshall, 1999; McCold, 2000; 2004; Ptacek, 2010; Zernova & Wright, 2007)?

The other theme is largely evaluative, focusing on whether restorative justice accomplishes what it sets out to do. This area of research tends to ask questions like: Does restorative justice work, is it more effective than conventional justice, does it achieve its situational and structural goals, who participates in restorative justice processes, are participants satisfied with restorative justice, is it useful or appropriate in specific types of situations or specific types of offenses, and does it address and work to tear down dominating structures (Coates & Gehm, 1989; Department of Justice, 2015; Larsen, 2014; Latimer, Dowden, & Muise, 2005; Maxwell, 2005; Maxwell, Kingi, Robertson, Morris, and Cunningham, 2004; McCold & Wachtel, 2002; Roberts, 2010; Vanfraechem, 2005; Weatherburn & Macadam, 2013; Wemmers, 2002)? These questions are important to consider as restorative justice evolves from a process-oriented framework within the realm of criminal justice into more modern conceptualizations primarily as a structuralist, ideological framework that permeates everyday life and conflict (Bazemore, O'Brien, & Carey, 2006).

This evolution raises several questions. For example, does the variety of conceptualizations of restorative justice problematize the generalizability and utility of research methods and findings? Is it possible to generalize from proceduralist research to structuralist practice, and vice versa? What exactly counts as "effective" if we define and enact restorative justice differently? These are important questions to tackle as research continues to evolve into what Hansen and Umbreit (2018) term "second-wave research" on restorative justice.

As we draw this text to a close and look ahead to what may be next, one of our aims is to address those questions by advancing a threefold argument. First, the study and practice of restorative justice should inform one another. Separating them can lead to problems of talking *past* one another rather than productively *engaging* one another (Hansen & Umbreit, 2018). Second, in light of what we have shown regarding the proceduralist and structuralist orientations of restorative justice, studying restorative justice from within and across multiple frameworks can enhance our practice and understanding of restorative processes, outcomes, and meanings individually, relationally, organizationally, and societally. Third, a communication perspective of restorative justice can help highlight the social and critical implications of restorative work, drawing our attention to the inherently personal and political experiences of restoration, relationships, and community and the structural consequences of those experiences (Paul & Borton, 2017).

Our other aim is to advocate for the importance of studying and researching restorative justice. Research can and should play a key role in advancing theory and practice, regardless of orientation to restorative justice. It calls us to be critically (self-)reflexive and examine the bases of the oft-times ideological assertions being made, with an eye toward data in all its forms. To explore these arguments and advance these aims, we first discuss conventional examinations of restorative justice before turning our attention to interpretive and critical approaches to studying restorative justice. We conclude with a series of questions designed to reflect on how we all can partner together to advance the research, theory, and practice of restorative justice.

CONVENTIONAL APPROACHES TO
STUDYING RESTORATIVE JUSTICE

The focus on defining, describing, and evaluating restorative justice has aimed to give structure and substance to an amorphous, emergent concept. As it blossomed in the West in the context of a conventional justice system that was quite different, a key question has been (and continues to be) about conceptualization—what is restorative justice? How does it differ from conventional justice? What does it look like? How is it done? The effort to define and describe restorative justice, such as through seminal work like Zehr's (1990) *Changing Lenses*, helped to stimulate theorizing about justice, particularly in light of the various concerns about conventional justice practices and consequences. Evaluative research helped to answer the next question—did it work as it claimed to (Kurki, 2003)? Was it better than the ways justice was typically done (Bergseth & Bouffard, 2007; Calhoun & Pelech, 2013; Gabbay, 2005; Latimer et al., 2001; Lipsey, 1995; Vanfraechem, 2005)? As a whole, this work reflected the proceduralist, instrumentalist roots of restorative justice in the West, as restorative justice was typically approached as a process or program to be implemented within the criminal justice system for the purposes of attaining particular (usually conventional) outcomes (Paul & Borton, 2017). These proceduralist roots, combined with the expectations and assumptions of conventional social science research, influenced the field's focus on a handful of (quantifiable) variables and to the use of variable-analytic methods to explore effectiveness as goal attainment (Cameron, 1978; Sheehan, 1996).

Evaluative research has typically focused on outcome variables for victims and offenders, particularly satisfaction (Bolívar, 2010; Bonta et al., 2002; Braithwaite, 2002; Coates & Gehm, 1989; Dignan, 2005; Johnstone, 2001; Kurki, 2003; Larsen, 2014; McCold, 2003; Rugge & Cormier, 2005; Shapland, Robinson, & Sorsby, 2011; Strang et al., 2006; Umbreit et al., 2004, 2008; van Camp & Wemmers, 2013; Van Ness & Schiff, 2001; Weatherburn & Macadam, 2013) and recidivism (Johnstone, 2001; Latimer et al., 2005; Rodriguez, 2007; Umbreit et al., 2004). Within this research, the focus has largely been on effects for victims, as noted in a report by Canada's Department of Justice (2015) that an "obvious definition of a successful program" was that it met "the needs of victims," especially "the satisfaction levels of victims in the traditional system compared to a restorative program." For victims, the primary outcome variables have been satisfaction (Kurki, 2003; Latimer et al., 2005), participation (Borton, 2009; Paul, 2015; Paul & Schenck-Hamlin, 2018), restitution / reparation (Bonta et al., 2002; Braithwaite, 2002; Dignan, 2005; Latimer et al., 2005; Paul, 2016; Shapland et al., 2006; Umbreit et al., 2004; Van Ness & Schiff, 2001; Zernova, 2007), and healing (Armour & Umbreit, 2006; Shapland et al., 2006; Umbreit et al., 2004; Zehr & Mika, 2010). Additional variables studied, as noted in Paul and Borton (2017), have included forgiveness (Armour & Umbreit, 2006; Braithwaite, 2016; Chapman & Chapman, 2016), empowerment (McCold, 2000; Morrison, 2006), and the receipt of additional information about the offense (Paul, 2015a; Zehr & Mika, 2010). There also has been a line of research focused on community impact and integration, including cost effectiveness (Gabbay, 2007) and assumptions about restorative justice (Paul & Schenck-Hamlin, 2017b). In all, these variables align within the framework of conventional Western justice.

Those same proceduralist, objectivist expectations also are apparent in the methodologies used. Much as Canada's Department of Justice (2015) report noted, the use of experimental designs and other quantitative designs have been predominant in conventional evaluations of restorative justice. The gold standard in (post-)positivist research design is the full experimental design that includes a control group and random assignment of participants (e.g., Shapland et al., 2007). Bergseth and Bouffard (2007) and Rodriguez (2007), though, note that both full and quasi-experimental designs experience design validity issues, including self-selection bias. Other research approaches, including survey research, lab experiments using vignettes, and analysis of organizational data (e.g., Borton, 2009; Paul, 2015; Paul & Schenck-Hamlin, 2018; Paul & Swan, 2018; Wenzel, Okimoto, & Cameron, 2012; Witvliet et al., 2007), also have contributed to research insights on attitudes toward and effects of restorative justice.

The use of these variable-analytic methods has a number of strengths. One is that they allow for systematic comparison between restorative justice procedures and conventional justice procedures in terms of process characteristics and outcomes. This helps to shed light on how observed outcomes may be tied to procedural elements of restorative justice processes that are distinct from those used in conventional justice processes. Highlighting these procedural elements can be useful for training and practice, as facilitators can utilize these findings to improve their work with victims, offenders, and other stakeholders. Another strength is the ability to control for intervening or extraneous factors that might influence the outcomes. For example, offense-related characteristics may influence willingness to participate in a restorative justice process (Paul, 2015). Statistical analyses, such as analysis of covariance, hierarchical linear regression, structural equation modeling, and moderation analysis, have the ability to control for these variables and to observe the effects. A third strength is that the production of quantitative findings using variable-analytic methods is rhetorically and politically advantageous. For example, Davis' (2018) discussion of the effectiveness of the restorative justice work in the Oakland School District highlights quantifiable outcomes, such as graduation rates, academic scores, chronic absences, and suspension rates, as indicators of effectiveness. Such highlighting fits with dominant Western narratives that actionable knowledge should be objective, impersonal, quantifiable, generalizable, and a product of the scientific method in order to be legitimate and acceptable. This has political implications as well, as making restorative justice take on a particular (conventional) appearance can be seen as a rhetorical strategy designed to increase its standing and legitimacy (Tassie, Murray, & Cutt, 1998; Yuchtman & Seashore, 1967). Essentially, the use of (post-)positivist methods helps to legitimize the practice of restorative justice by drawing on conventional social scientific and evaluative discourses and methods.

Having said that, such methods also have a number of limitations. For one, they are less effective than interpretive methods at addressing structural and communicative elements of restorative justice. As demonstrated by Rossner's (2013) exploration of emotions in victim-offender mediation, methods such as conversation analysis can highlight the communicative practices that constitute restorative justice processes. Additionally, researchers have highlighted the importance of examining narrative to reveal constructions of justice and underlying problems of domination, alienation, and oppression (Giles, 2019; González, 2015). For another, the underlying assumption of generalizability may be problematic, as restorative justice programs and processes frequently vary by context (McAlister & Carr, 2014). Meanings associated with symbols like "restorative justice," "victim-offender mediation," and "dialogue" might influence, for example, support for restorative justice and behavior during restorative justice processes (Borton & Paul, 2015). A third limitation is the lack of adequate valid measures that have been rigorously evaluated. Rather than developing a measure with adequate content validity of, for example, satisfaction, items are used that measure satisfaction *generally* (Bolívar, 2010; Presser & van Voorhis, 2002). It is difficult and problematic to draw specific conclusions based on general data derived from global measures. A fourth limitation concerns the preoccupation with certain outcome variables like satisfaction and recidivism. As noted elsewhere (Paul & Borton, 2017), focusing primarily on outcomes of satisfaction and recidivism neglects the other ostensible outcomes of restorative justice, including closure, growth, empowerment, and relationship repair (Braithwaite, 1999; Johnstone, 2001; Morris, 2002; Paul & Dunlop, 2014; Umbreit et al., 2004; Zehr, 2002b).

In all, restorative justice research that has focused on conceptualizing, describing, and evaluating has been important for providing a foundation upon which to begin exploring restorative justice. The use of variable-analytic methods to explore questions of participation and effects has enhanced our understanding of how restorative justice features influence people's experience of restorative processes. Yet, its limitations, combined with the

structuralist shift, also call for other approaches to studying restorative justice. These other approaches, including interpretive and critical approaches,
are rooted in a communicative perspective of restorative justice that highlights questions of language, structure, power, and meaning best explored
through qualitative research methods.

INTERPRETIVE AND CRITICAL APPROACHES
TO STUDYING RESTORATIVE JUSTICE

In discussing interpretive and critical approaches, we do not claim that variable-analytic, quantitative studies are ineffective, unwarranted, or inappropriate. Instead, we claim that interpretive and critical approaches to research are
likely more effective at examining questions pertaining to the communicative,
structural, and systemic underpinnings of the social construct of restorative
justice. By examining communicative patterns and practices, including narrative and meaning making, we can explore the emergence and intersections
of systems, structures, and symbols that constitute restorative justice (Giles,
2019; González 2015).

The use of interpretive and critical approaches aligns with a communicative constitution perspective of restorative justice in several ways (see Paul
& Borton, 2017). First, it frames restorative justice as a social construct situated within contexts, constituted through language, and emergent over time
(Paul, 2016). This framing accounts for differences in how people understand
and practice restorative justice, whether doing so procedurally or structurally. Language and interaction take center stage with this perspective, as
they make restorative justice what it is. Second, and related, it aligns with a
perspective that frames justice as negotiated, situated, and emergent (Paul,
2015b; Paul & Borton, 2017; Vaandering, 2011; Warnke, 1992). From this
perspective, justice is a product of socialization over time by multiple parties
(Humby, 2014). Third, given its axiological commitments of highlighting
the values of researchers, it draws attention to the ideological foundations
of restorative justice. All of us—whether we are researchers, practitioners,
observers, participants, or otherwise—bring our own ideologies to the table
when interpreting and practicing restorative justice. Interpretive and critical research asks evaluators to bring to the surface their own values, norms,
beliefs, and attitudes when studying restorative justice (Creswell, 2013).
Davis (2019), for example, demonstrates this upfront surfacing in *The Little
Book of Race and Restorative Justice*. Fourth, in line with its attention to
underlying ideologies, interpretive and critical frameworks align with a
social justice research perspective that identifies power systems and works to

emancipate people from oppressive unjust systems. For example, communication activism scholarship:

> involves communication researchers . . . using their theories, methods, and applied practices to work with and for oppressed, marginalized, and underresourced groups and communities . . . as well as activist groups and organizations . . . to intervene into unjust discourses and material conditions to make them more just, and documenting and reporting their practices, processes, and effects to multiple publics. (Carragee & Frey, 2016, pp. 3975–3976)

Such scholarship is consistent with calls for restorative justice practitioners and researchers to pursue social justice and social change aims (Davis, 2018; 2019; González, 2015; Opie & Roberts, 2017; Pranis, 2001; Winslade, 2019).

These approaches lead to a number of questions that can expand our understanding, practice, and evaluation of restorative justice. On an individual level, we might explore how people define concepts like "restoration" and "justice," as Paul and Schenck-Hamlin (2017) and Paul and Borton (2013) did. This should include examining how such constructions are situated within larger meaning systems and how they come to those constructions, and how those definitions might change over time. Research also can explore how people make sense of their experience within restorative processes, leading to more sensitive, nuanced, and ultimately powerful evaluations of restorative justice processes. Analytical methods such as discourse analysis (Fairhurst & Putnam, 2014; Phillips & Jorgensen, 2011; Phillips, Lawrence, & Hardy, 2004), thematic analysis (Braun & Clarke, 2006), and grounded theory (Corbin & Strauss, 1990), combined with methods such as interviewing (e.g., Bolivar, 2012), focus groups, and participant observation, can be useful for highlighting these constructions and situating them in context.

On a relational level, we might examine characteristics of interaction during restorative processes like victim-offender mediation and family group conferencing, much as Rossner (2013) did. Using conversation analysis, ethnography of communication, and participant observation can draw attention to how participants' negotiate outcomes, power, and values through their communicative exchanges. By examining interaction, we become more attuned to how people experience and interpret restorative processes. This can serve to break the problematic presumption that methods are neutral, and instead invites researchers and practitioners to pay more attention to how the interaction of all parties—facilitators, primary stakeholders, and secondary stakeholders—negotiate and accomplish restoration.

On a wider structural level, methods such as rhetorical criticism, narrative analysis, critical ethnography, and discourse analysis can facilitate an exploration of how discourses of restorative justice are tied in with other social discourses, the larger institutionalizing of restorative justice, and the structural influence of restorative justice (Phillips et al., 2004). Discourse analytic methods can explore points of connection and disconnection with, for example, conventional justice discourses, social movement rhetoric, and discourses from other cultures to understand the evolution of our practice of restorative justice. Narrative analysis, in turn, can clarify the dynamics by which relational and societal narratives constitute justice, in line with the theory of justicecraft (Giles, 2019). This perspective draws attention to the symbolic nature of justice and the ways in which it is implicated in our day-to-day discourses and larger narratives that implicate identity, status, and belonging, as foregrounded by perspectives like coordinated management of meaning (Pearce & Pearce, 2000). In turn, such approaches, drawing on perspectives such as communication activism, critical race theory, feminist theory, and queer theory, can show the ways in which restorative justice transforms or perhaps paradoxically reinforces conventional justice by high-lighting and problematizing ideological foundations.

This understanding and situating can facilitate the pursuit of transfor-mative and emancipatory aims inherent in a structuralist orientation to restorative justice. Echoing similar refrains as Carragee and Frey (2016), González (2015) argues that "restorative justice should be re-theorized as a way to confront injustice that becomes a political demand, specifically one for emancipation, for an end to domination and oppression, and the right to have a meaningful, rather than tokenized voice" (p. 460). One way this can be done is to highlight narratives that perpetuate conventional construc-tions of justice that result in alienation and domination. For example, Schiff (2018) highlights the need to "dismantle cultural narratives and structures that celebrate exclusion and punishment as just responses to harm, over com-passionate restorative responses to keep youth in school, off the streets and out of the justice system" (p. 134). Likewise, using critical race theory as a lens through which to explore restorative justice can "reveal the oppressive underbelly of dominant discourse that processes false commitment to racial equality, neutrality, objectivity, meritocracy and justice" (Griffin, 2010, p. 3). Similarly, feminist theories can highlight the ways in which conventional and restorative justice processes, practices, and discourses implicate gender con-structions and the politics associated with gender identity (Anderson, 2016; Daly & Stubbs, 2006; 2007).

In all, the use of interpretive and critical approaches can expand our understanding and evaluation of restorative justice. It draws attention to the ways in which restorative justice is situated in, influences, and is influenced by individual, relational, and cultural contexts, coinciding with structuralist framings of restorative justice. Given that, we conclude by offering a few recommendations for researchers and practitioners going forward.

IMPLICATIONS, RECOMMENDATIONS, AND CONTINUED PROGRESS

As both researchers and practitioners, we approach the study of restorative justice with a particular appreciation for data, research, and practice. As communication scholars who have been trained in both qualitative and quantitative research, as well as practitioners and researchers of conflict management and mediation, we are keenly interested in not only instrumental approaches to communication (i.e., how people communicate) but also constitutive approaches to communication (i.e., what communication creates). We also are firm believers in the ideal that research and practice should co-exist, inform, and advance one another, and that curiosity, questions, and dialogue can inspire new ideas and thinking about restorative justice. Indeed, it is in the spirit of dialogue with which we offer this co-authored work. From this perspective we offer the following questions for consideration.

First, what would happen to the quality of our studies and programs if researchers and practitioners worked toward developing long-term, stable, and mutually beneficial partnerships? This question draws on the traditions of pragmatism and engaged scholarship. The pragmatic perspective argues for the need for ethical research to *do* something—to benefit stakeholders, to facilitate meaningful change, and to advance work. In engaged scholarship, we argue that the development of collaborative partnerships between researchers and practitioners can most effectively accomplish that benefitting, meaningful change, and advancement. The engaged perspective (Barge & Shockley-Zalabak, 2008; Connaughton et al., 2017; Dempsey & Barge, 2013) focuses on the importance of researcher-practitioner partnerships that co-construct questions, co-design methods, and evaluate and interpret findings together. Working toward creating such partnerships can help to repair the needless and problematic divide between research and practice. As practitioners wonder about the utility and benefits of scholarship, researchers wonder about whether practitioners are making evidence-based decisions. Developing and maintaining partnerships will take energy, ongoing conversation, and the successful management of natural tensions that arise (Paul, 2020). Yet, it holds promise for advancing both research and practice in restorative justice.

There are numerous opportunities for engaged research in school settings, family settings, and community settings. In school settings, as teachers, counselors, and administrators grapple with issues such as cyberbullying, problematic home environments, and the systemic consequences of zero-tolerance practices, there are opportunities for researchers to join with educators to develop evidence-based accountability systems within a broader whole-school restorative practices framework to achieve goals related to anti-racism, improved learning, the elimination of the school-to-prison pipeline,

positive youth development, fuller parental involvement in children's learning, and more constructive organizational environments. In community settings, as modeled by Connaughton and team's Purdue Peace Project, there
also are opportunities to use research approaches such as community-based
participatory research to make progress on community-wide initiatives connected with restorative values and practices. Such work would involve more
than a once-and-done event or a series of interviews with community members (Paul, 2020). Instead, it would necessitate likely a group of researchers,
organizational stakeholders, and community stakeholders meeting and col-
laborating to identify goals, processes, and methods for accomplishing both
short- and long-term change. Studies could broaden to consider the larger
systems in which they are operating (see chapter 5) in order to make progress
on accomplishing such change. They would then need to be reflexive and
attentive to constraints and opportunities connected with the immediate situation and the larger systems as they pursue their goals. Prudent practicioners
and researchers will understand that alterations made to systems will have
perhaps unexpected consequences in other parts of the system.

Second, and in line with the advocacy for researcher-practitioner partnerships, what would happen to our study and conceptualization of restorative
justice if we utilized multiple and mixed approaches? Mixed-methods and
multi-method approaches can address the limitations inherent in both methods and highlight their strengths. We do not argue that one approach is
superior to the other. Instead, we argue that they can generate questions best
addressed together. For example, Paul and Schenck-Hamlin (2018) used a
survey method in which they asked participants a series of open-ended questions, including what came to mind when hearing "restorative justice." They
used content analysis to identify patterns and frequencies, finding that words
like "restoration" and "justice" were most frequently identified. A potential
follow-up to this type of analysis would be to conduct either individual interviews or focus groups, using a sampling method that aimed to diversify participants, to drill down into how people interpreted those terms and to explore
how those interpretations coincided with their other values. This approach
can work the other way as well, following up interview-generated findings
with experiments or surveys that examined the effects or relationships associated with different conceptualizations of restorative justice. Either way,
the pairing of methods, whether using data triangulation or methodological
triangulation, can advance restorative justice research while speaking to the
varied interests of stakeholders.

Such mixed-methods work can be especially helpful with emerging practices in digital spaces. While the "low-hanging fruit" that is easily picked for
analysis may simply be the rate and characteristics of agreements (e.g., restitution), participation satisfaction, and other conventional measures rather easily

assessed through conventional quantitative approaches to research, other practices such as participant observation and interviewing can add depth and answer questions related to communication practices, identity, meaning, and framing. For example, Rossner's (2013) qualitative investigation of emotion rituals exemplifies the type of investigative work that researchers can conduct regarding participants' communication practices in digital spaces. Likewise, mixed methods research can help schools move beyond quantitative metrics to gauge effectiveness of restorative interventions to also examine, for example, how students and teachers talk about conflict, community, and school/organizational citizenship.

Third, what can we accomplish with variables that are more clearly operationalized and measures that have been appropriately and rigorously tested? While existing research has advanced our understanding of restorative justice outcomes, one concern is that measures of those outcomes lack sufficient content validity. This means that they do not get at all the relevant dimensions of the variable being measured. Satisfaction, for example, has multiple dimensions—satisfaction with material outcomes, with relational outcomes, with emotional outcomes, with processes, with facilitator communication, or with offender communication. While multidimensional measures may be unwieldy as post-process effectiveness assessments, they provide much richer detail and information to practitioners about what worked and what did not. The development of valid and reliable measures requires clear operationalization of variables, and is an important next step in the quantitative study of restorative justice. Our hope is that the structuralist turn of restorative justice does not marginalize quantitative investigations that dig into the mechanics and outcomes of restorative processes. In line with our aforementioned question, we argue that all methods can contribute meaningfully to the various aims of restorative justice associated with proceduralist and structuralist orientations.

Fourth, to what extent are we willing to engage in critical reflections on restorative justice and ourselves? It is important for all of us—researchers, practitioners, participants, scholars and observers—to ask difficult questions about restorative justice processes and outcomes and our roles in making restorative justice what it is. For example, Choi, Bazemore, and Gilbert (2012) note that "outliers" of negative experiences in restorative justice can improve and inform the practice of restorative justice and are in need of continued examination. Likewise, research, such as that by Daly and Stubbs (2006), van Wormer (2009), and Ptacek (2010), interrogates the appropriateness of using restorative processes and practices in situations involving intimate and relational violence. We are concerned that people beg the question of restorative justice's appropriateness and effectiveness, simply assuming that restorative justice is an inherent good. This assumption can have the (un) intended effect of suppressing critical questions all of us must be mindful of: good for whom, under what conditions, when, and in what ways? What makes restorative justice good, and are there situations in which restorative justice is not good? Does the adoption of a restorative framework perpetuate an ideological conflict in which people who are uncertain of restorative justice or who do not engage in restorative practices are marginalized or shunned? Could the adoption of restorative justice as a value (e.g., see Fehr and Gelfand's [2012] model of the forgiving organization) (un)intentionally pressure people into meeting with, forgiving, or reconciling with someone with whom they do not feel safe? We must create space for asking difficult questions of restorative justice and ourselves, avoiding the pull to re-create a polarized us/them scenario that ironically succeeds in marginalizing the very others we wish to see included.

The investigation of restorative justice provides opportunities to make progress on a number of fronts. Post-positive, interpretive, and critical approaches can be used to explore areas that are of interest to researchers and practitioners from proceduralist and structuralist orientations. Additionally, approaches to research such as engaged scholarship and activism/social justice scholarship can advance both the theory and practice of restorative justice. Our hope is that restorative justice research will facilitate transformation and empowerment for individuals, relationships, workplaces, communities, and beyond.

A CONCLUDING THOUGHT

We began this journey by asking a number of questions brought to the fore by highlighting the role of communication in constituting restorative justice. In addition to serving as a vehicle for the exchange of ideas and information, communication lies at the heart of the human experience, giving meaning to ourselves, our relationships, our experiences, and our communities. It is at the heart of the stories we tell, the arguments we make, the processes and programs we run, the moral systems we live by, the relationships we manage, and the social systems we aim to create. It is at the heart of justice.

We continue to believe that restorative justice offers a socially just framework within which to pursue fairness in our schools, our families, our communities, and our workplaces. Whether we primarily approach restorative justice from a proceduralist perspective that pays primary attention to processes and programs or from a structuralist perspective that hews more toward structural and systems change, we know that the work we pursue is rooted in complex and always-emerging ideological webs with deep histories, rich vocabularies, and intriguing possibilities. These approaches are not mutually exclusive; in fact, they are mutually edifying, as systems, structures, and practices are inextricably linked. It is through continued collaboration and dialogue among practitioners, researchers, and community stakeholders that we can pursue restoration together.

REFERENCES

Anderson, P. S. (2016). When justice and forgiveness come apart: A feminist perspective on restorative justice and intimate violence. *Oxford Journal of Law and Religion, 5*, 113–134. https://doi.org/10.1093/ojlr/rww002.

Armour, M. P., & Umbreit, M. S. (2006). Victim forgiveness in restorative justice dialogue. *Victim and Offenders, 1*(2), 123–140. https://doing.org/10.10.1080/1 5564880600626080.

Bazemore, G. & Walgrave, L. (1999). Restorative justice: In search of fundamentals. In G. Bazemore & L. Walgrave (Eds.), *Restorative juvenile justice: Repairing the harm of youth crime* (pp. 45–74). Criminal Justice Press.

Bazemore, G., O'Brien, S., & Carey, M. (2006). The synergy and substance of organizational and community change in the response to crime and conflict: The emergence and potential of restorative justice. *Public Organization Review: A Global Journal, 5*, 287–314. https://doi.org/.

Bergseth, K. J., & Bouffard, J. A. (2007). The long-term impact of restorative justice programming for juvenile offenders. *Journal of Criminal Justice, 35*(4), 433–451. https://doi.org/10.1016/j.jcrimjus.2007.05.006.

Bolívar, D. (2010). Conceptualizing victims' "restoration" in restorative justice. *International Review of Victimology, 17*(3), 237–265. https://doi.org/10.1177/0 26975801001700301.

Bonta, J., Wallace-Capretta, S., Rooney, J., & McAnoy, K. (2002). An outcome evaluation of a restorative justice alternative to incarceration. *Contemporary Justice Review, 5*(4), 319–338. https://doi.org/10.1080/10282580214772.

Borton, I. M. (2009). Effects of race, sex, and victims' reasons for victim-offender dialogue. *Conflict Resolution Quarterly, 27*(2), 215–235. https://doi.org/10.1002/crq.256.

Borton, I. M., & Paul, G. D. (2015). Problematizing the healing metaphor of restorative justice. *Contemporary Justice Review, 18*(3), 257–273. https://doi.org/10.1 080/10282580.2015.1057704.

Bradshaw, W., & Roseborough, D., & Umbreit (2006). The effect of victim offender mediation on juvenile offender recidivism: A meta-analysis. *Conflict Resolution Quarterly, 24*(1), 87–98. https://doi.org/10.1002/crq.159.

Braithwaite, J. (1999). Restorative justice: Assessing optimistic and pessimistic accounts in M. Tonry (ed.). *Crime and justice: A review of research* (vol. 25, pp. 1–127). University of Chicago Press. https://doi.org/449287.

Braithwaite, J. (2002). Setting standards for restorative justice. *British Journal of Criminology, 42*(3), 563–577. https://doi.org/10. 1093/bjc/42.3.563.

Braithwaite, J. (2016). Redeeming the "F" word in restorative justice. *Oxford Journal of Law and Religion, 5*(1), 79–93. https://doi.org/10.1093/ojlr/rwv049.

Calhoun, A., & Pelech, W. (2013). The impact of restorative and conventional responses to harm on victims: A comparative study. *British Journal of Community Justice, 11*(1), 63–84. https://doi.org/10.1080/10282580.2010.498238.

Cameron, K. S. (1978). Measuring organizational effectiveness in institutions of higher education. *Administrative Science Quarterly, 23*(4), 604–632. https://doi.org/10.2307/2392582.

Chapman, T., & Chapman, A. (2016). Forgiveness in restorative justice: Experienced but not heard? *Oxford Journal of Law and Religion, 5*(1), 135–152. https://doi.org/10.1093/ojlr/rwv066.

Choi, J. J., Bazemore, G., & Gilbert, M. J. (2012). Review of research on victims' experiences in restorative justice: Implications for youth justice. *Children and Youth Services Review, 34*(1), 35–42. https://doi.org/10.1016/j.childyouth.2011.08.011.

Coates, R. B., & Gehm, J. (1989). An empirical assessment. In M. Wright & B. Galaway (Eds.), *Mediation and criminal justice: Victims, offenders and community* (pp. 251–263). Sage.

Creswell, J. W. (2013). *Qualitative inquiry and research design: Choosing among five approaches* (3rd ed.). Sage.

Daly, K. (2016). What is restorative justice? Fresh answers to a vexed question. *Victims & Offenders, 11*(1), 9–29. https://doi.org/10.1080/15564886.2015.1107797.

Daly, K., & Stubbs J. (2007). Feminist theory, feminist and anti-racist politics, and restorative justice. In G. Johnstone & D. Van Ness (Eds.), *Handbook of restorative justice* (pp. 149–170). Willan.

Daly, K., & Stubbs J. (2006). Feminist engagement with restorative justice. *Theoretical Criminology, 10*(1), 9–28. https://doi.org/10.1177/1362480606059980.

Davis, F. E. (2019). *The little book of race and restorative justice: Black lives, healing, and US social transformation*. Good Books.

Davis, F. E. (2018). Whole school restorative justice as a racial justice and liberatory practice: Oakland's journey. *The International Journal of Restorative Justice, 1*(3), 428–432. https://doi.org/10.5553/IJRJ/258908912018001003007.

Department of Justice (2015). The effects of restorative justice programming: A review of the empirical. http://www.justice.gc.ca/eng/rp-pr/csj-sjc/jsp-sjp/rr00_16/p3.html.

Dignan, J. (2005). Evaluating restorative justice from a victim perspective—Empirical evidence. In C. Hoyle (Ed.), *Restorative justice: Critical concepts in criminology* (pp. 3–35). Routledge.

Doolin, C. (2007). But what does it mean? Seeking definitional clarity in restorative justice. *The Journal of Criminal Law, 71*(5), 427–440. https://doi.org/10.1350/jcla.2007.71.5.427.

Fehr, R., & Gelfand, M. J. (2012). The forgiving organization: A multilevel model of forgiveness at work. *Academy of Management Review, 37*(4), 664–688. https://doi.org/10.5465/amr.2010.0497.

Gabbay, Z. D. (2005). Justifying restorative justice: A theoretical justification for the use of restorative justice practices. *Journal of Dispute Resolution, 2*(2), 349–397. https://heinonline.org/HOL/P?h=hein.journals/jdisres2005&i=355.

Griffin, R. A. (2010). Critical race theory as a means to deconstruction, recover and evolve in communication studies. *Communication Law Review, 10*(1), http://www .commlawreview.org/Archives/CLRv10i1/PDFs/Critical_Race_Theory_as_a_Me ans_to_Deconstruct_Recover_and_Evolve_in_Communication_Studies.pdf.

Hansen, T., & Umbreit, M. (2018). State of knowledge: Four decades of victim-offender mediation research and practice: The evidence. *Conflict Resolution Quarterly, 36*(2), 99–113. https://doi.org/10.1002/crq.21234.

Hill, F. D. (2008). Restorative justice: Sketching a new legal discourse. *International Journal of Punishment and Sentencing, 4*(2), 51–81. https://heinonline.org/HOL/P ?h=hein.journals/punisen4&i=59.

Humby, T. L. (2014). Redressing mining legacies: The case of the south African mining industry. *Journal of Business Ethics, 135,* 653–664. https://doi.org/10.1007 /s10551-014-2380-8.

Johnstone, G. (2001). *Restorative justice: Ideas, values, debates.* Willan.

Kurki, L. (2003). Evaluating restorative justice practices. In A. von Hirsch, J. Roberts, A. Bottoms, K. Roach, & M. Schiff (Eds.), *Restorative justice and criminal justice: Competing or reconcilable paradigms?* (pp. 293–314). Hart.

Larsen, J. J. (2014). Restorative justice in the Australian criminal justice system. Report prepared for the Australian Institute of Criminology. http://www.aic.gov.a u/media_library/publications/rpp/rpp127.pdf.

Latimer, J., Dowden, C., & Muise, D. (2005). The effectiveness of restorative justice practices: A meta-analysis. *The Prison Journal, 85*(2), 127–144. https://doi.org/10 .1177/0032885505276969.

Lipsey, M. (1995). What do we learn from 400 research studies on effectiveness of treatment with juvenile delinquents? In J. McGuire (Ed.), *What works: Reducing reoffending- Guidelines from research and practice* (pp. 63–78). Wiley.

Marshall, T. F. (1999). *Restorative justice: An overview.* Home Office, Research Development and Statistics Directorate.

Maxwell, G. (2005). Achieving effective outcomes in youth justice: Implications of new research for principals, policy, and practice. In E. Elliot & R. M. Gordon (Eds.), *New directions in restorative justice: Issues, practice, evaluation* (pp. 53–74). Willan.

Maxwell, G., Kingi, V., Robertson, J., Morris, A., & Cunningham, C. (2004). Achieving effective outcomes in youth justice: Final report. New Zealand Ministry of Justice, Wellington. https://www.msd.govt.nz/documents/about-msd-and-our -work/publications-resources/archive/2004-achieving-effective-outcomes-youth-ju stice-full-report.pdf.

McAlister, S. & Carr, N. (2014). Experiences of youth justice: Youth justice dis-courses and their multiple effects. *Youth Justice, 14*(3), 241–254. https://doi.org /10.1177/1473225414549694.

McCold, P., & Wachtel, T. (2002). Restorative justice theory validation. In E. G. M. Weitekamp & H-J. Kerner (Eds.), *Restorative justice: Theoretical foundations* (pp. 110–142). Willan.

McCold, P. (2000). Toward a holistic vision of restorative juvenile justice: A reply to the maximalist model. *Contemporary Justice Review, 3*, 35–414.

McCold, P. (2003). A survey assessment research on mediation and conferencing. In L. Walgrave (Ed.), *Repositioning restorative justice* (pp. 67–120). Willan.

McCold, P. (2004). Paradigm muddle: The threat to restorative justice posed by its merger with community justice. *Contemporary Justice Review, 7*(1), 13–35. https://doi.org/10.1080/1028258042000211987.

Morris, A. (2002). Critiquing the critics: A brief response to critics of restorative justice. *British Journal of Criminology, 42*(3), 596–615. https://doi.org/10.1093/bjc/42.3.596.

Morrison, B. (2006). School bullying and restorative justice: Toward a theoretical understanding of the role of respect, pride, and shame. *Journal of Social Issues, 62*(2), 371–392. https://doi.org/10.1111/j.1540-4560.2006.00455.x.

Mullane, R., Burrell, N. A., Allen, M., & Timmerman, L. (2014). Victim-offender mediation: A meta-analysis. In N. Burrell, M. Allen, B. M. Gayle, & R. W. Preiss (Eds.), *Managing interpersonal conflict: Advances through meta-analysis* (pp. 106–124). Routledge.

Opie, T., Roberts, L. M. (2017). Do black lives really matter in the workplace? Restorative justice as a means to reclaim humanity. *Equality, Diversity, and Inclusion, 36*(8), 707–719. https://doi.org/10.1108/EDI-07-2017-0149.

Paul, G. D. (2015a). Predicting participation in victim offender conferences. *Negotiation and Conflict Management Research, 8*(2), 100–118. https://doi.org/10.1111/ncmr.12049.

Paul, G. D. (2016). A bona fide group perspective of restorative justice: Implications for researchers and practitioners. In P. M. Kellett & T. G. Matyok (Eds.), *Transforming conflict through communication in personal, family, and workplace relationships* (pp. 125–130). Lexington Books.

Paul, G. D., & Borton, I. M. (2013). Exploring communities of facilitators: Orientations toward restorative justice. *Conflict Resolution Quarterly, 31*(2), 189–218. https://doi.org/10.1002/crq.21073.

Paul, G. D., & Borton, I. M. (2017). Toward a communication perspective of restorative justice: Implications for research, facilitation, and assessment. *Negotiation and Conflict Management Research, 10*(3), 199–219. https://doi.org/10.1111/ncmr.12097.

Paul, G. D., & Schenck-Hamlin, W. (2017). Beliefs about victim-offender conferences: Factors influencing victim-offender engagement. *Conflict Resolution Quarterly, (1), 47–72. https://doi.org/10.1002/crq.21190.

Paul, G. D., & Swan, E. C. (2018). Receptivity to restorative justice: A survey of goal importance, process effectiveness, and support for victim-offender conferencing. *Conflict Resolution Quarterly, 36*(2), 145–162. https://doi.org/10.1002/crq.21238.

Pearce, W. B., & Pearce, K. A. (2000). Extending the theory of the coordinated management of meaning (CMM) through a community dialogue process. *Communication Theory, 10*(4), 405–423. https://doi.org/10.1111/j.468-2885.2000.tb00200.x.

Pranis, K. (2001). Restorative justice, social justice, and the empowerment of marginalized populations. In G. Bazemore & M. Schiff (Eds.), *Restorative community justice: Repairint harm and transforming communities* (pp. 287–306). Anderson Publishing Co.

Presser, L. & Van Voorhis, P. (2002). Values and evaluation: Assessing processes and outcomes of restorative justice programs. *Crime & Delinquency, 48*(1), 162–188. https://doi.org/10.1177/0011128702048001007.

Ptacek, J. (2010). Editor's introduction. In J. Ptacek (Ed.), *Restorative justice and violence against women* (pp. ix–xii). Oxford University Press.

Roberts, M. L. (2010). *Evaluating evaluation: An investigation into the purpose and practice of evaluation in restorative justice based programs.* [Unpublished master's thesis]. Simon Fraser University.

Rodriguez, N. (2007). Restorative justice at work: examining the impact of restorative justice resolutions on juvenile recidivism. *Crime and Delinquency, 53*(3), 355–379 https://doi.org/10.1177/0011128705285983.

Rossner, M. (2013). *Just emotions: Rituals of restorative justice.* Oxford UP.

Rugge, T. & Cormier, R. (2005). Restorative justice in cases of serious crime: an evaluation. In E. Elliot & R. M. Gordon (Eds.), *New directions in restorative justice: Issues, practice, evaluation* (pp. 266–277). Willan.

Shapland, J., Atkinson, A., Atkinson, H., College, E., Dignan, J., Howes, M., Johnstone, J., Robinson, G. & Sorsby, A. (2006). Situating restorative justice within criminal justice. *Theoretical Criminology, 10*(4), 505–532. https://doi.org /10.1177/1362480606068876.

Sheehan, R. B., Jr. (1996). Mission accomplishment as philanthropic organization effectiveness: Key findings from the excellence in philanthropy projects. *Nonprofit and Voluntary Sector Quarterly, 25*(1), 110–123. https://doi.org/10.1177/089976 4096251008.

Strang, H., Sherman, L. W., Angel, C. M., Woods, D. J., Bennett, S., Newbury-Birch, D., & Inkpen, N. (2006). Victim evaluations of face-to-face restorative justice conferences: A quasi-experimental analysis. *Journal of Social Issues, 62*(2), 281–306. https://doi.org/10.1111/j.1540-4560.2006.00451.x.

Tassie, B., Murray, V., & Cutt, J. (1998). Evaluating social service agencies: Fuzzy pictures of organizational effectiveness. *Voluntas, 9*, 59–79. https://doi.org/10 .1023/a:1021455029092.

Umbreit, M. S., Coates, R.B., & Vos, B. (2004). Victim-offender mediation: Three decades of practice and research. *Conflict Resolution Quarterly, 22*(2), 279–303. https://heinonline.org/HOL/P?h=hein.journals/cfltrq22&i=279.

Vaandering, D. (2011). A faithful compass: Rethinking the term restorative justice to find clarity. *Contemporary Justice Review, 14*(3), 307–328. https://doi.org/10.1080 /10282580.2011.589668.

van Camp, T., & Wemmers, J. (2013). Victim satisfaction with restorative justice: More than simply procedural justice. *International Review of Victimology, 19*(2), 117–143. https://doi.org/10.1177/0269758012472764.

Van Ness, D. W., & Schiff, M. F. (2001). Satisfaction guaranteed? The meaning of satisfaction in restorative justice. In G. Bazemore & M. F. Schiff (Eds.),

Restorative community justice: Repairing harm and transforming communities (pp. 47–62). Anderson.

Van Wormer, K. (2009). Restorative justice as social justice for victims of gendered violence: A standpoint feminist perspective. *Social Work, 54*(2), 107–116. https://doi.org/10.1093/sw/54.2.107.

Vanfraechem, I. (2005). Evaluating conferencing for serious juvenile offenders. In E. Elliot &

R. M. Gordon (Eds.), *New directions in restorative justice: Issues, practice, evaluation* (pp. 278–295). Willan.

Warnke, G. (1992). *Justice and interpretation*. MIT Press.

Weatherburn, D., & Macadam, M. (2013). A review of restorative justice responses to offending. https://journal.anzsog.edu.au/userfiles/files/EvidenceBase2013Issue1.pdf.

Wemmers, J. (2002). Restorative justice for victims of crime: A victim-oriented approach to restorative justice. *International Review of Victimology, 9*(1), 43–59. https://doi.org/10.1177/026975800200900104.

Wenzel, M., Okimoto, T. G., & Cameron, K. (2012). Do retributive and restorative justice processes address different symbolic concerns? *Critical Criminology, 20*, 25–44. https://doi.org/10.1007/s10612-011-9147-7.

Winslade, J. (2019). Can restorative justice promote social justice? *Contemporary Justice Review, 22*(3), 280–289. https://doi.org/10.1080/10282580.2019.1644173.

Witvliet, C. V. O., Worthington, E. L., Root, L. M., Sato, A. F., Ludwig, T. E., & Exline, J. J. (2008). Retributive justice, restorative justice, and forgiveness: An experimental psychophysiology analysis. *Journal of Experimental Social Psychology, 44*(1), 10–25. https://doi.org/10.1016/j.esp.2007.01.009.

Yuchtman, E., & Seashore, S. E. (1967). A system resource approach to organizational effectiveness. *American Sociological Review, 32*(6), 891–903. https://doi.org/10.2307/2092843.

Zehr, H. (1990). *Changing lenses: A new focus for crime and justice*. Herald Press.

Zehr, H. (2002b). Journey to belonging. In E. G. M. Weitekamp and H-J Kerner (Eds.), *Restorative justice: Theoretical foundations* (pp. 21–31). Willan.

Zehr H., & Mika, M. (2010). Fundamental concepts of restorative justice. In C. Hoyle (Ed.), *Restorative justice: Critical concepts in criminology* (pp. 57–64). Routledge.

Zernova, M. (2007). Aspirations of restorative justice proponents and experiences of participants in family group conferences. *British Journal of Criminology, 47*(3), 491–509. https://doi.org/10.1093/bjc.azl063.

Zernova, M. & Wright, M. (2007). Alternative visions of restorative justice. In G. Johnstone & D. W. Van Ness (Eds.), *Handbook of restorative justice* (pp. 91–108). Willan.

Index

About the Authors

Gregory D. Paul (PhD, Texas A&M University) is professor and head of the Department of Communication Studies at Kansas State University. His research examines the intersections of restorative justice, communication, and conflict management, with an interest in discourses of restorative justice and attitudes toward restorative justice.

Ian M. Borton (PhD, Bowling Green State University) is a professor of communication at Aquinas College in Grand Rapids, Michigan. He has been a restorative practitioner, researcher, advocate, mediator, and scholar since 2004. His research frequently combines restorative justice, communication, and conflict. Recently, he has been studying the use of gamification and role-play as pedagogy.

www.ingramcontent.com/pod-product-compliance
Lightning Source LLC
Chambersburg PA
CBHW022326280326
41932CB00010B/1247